Shift Your Perspective

Navigating Life Through Different Perspectives

Paras Panjwani

Contents

Note From the Author

This book is a collection of my personal viewpoints and ideas that have helped me see life differently. While research backs some perspectives, others come from personal experiences and observations. This isn't a rulebook or professional advice, just a way to explore new ways of thinking. Take what resonates with you, question what doesn't, and most importantly, make it your own.

Each perspective in this book is unique and stands on its own. The chapters don't follow a fixed sequence, you can read them in any order. There's no storyline to follow, just shifts in thinking that can happen at any moment.

Introduction

Have you ever felt stuck in a rut, unable to see beyond your current circumstances? Do you find yourself constantly battling negative thoughts and emotions, wondering if there's a better way to approach life? If so, you're not alone. In today's fast-paced world, it's all too easy to get caught up in our own perspectives, limiting our ability to see from a different perspective and find true happiness.

This book is especially for those who find themselves at a crossroads, whether it's in their career, relationships, or personal identity, and are searching for clarity, growth, and a deeper understanding of life. Whether you're facing a major life transition or simply seeking new ways to navigate everyday struggles, the insights in this book are designed to shift how you see the world and yourself.

Rather than offering surface-level motivation, this is a roadmap to personal growth and fulfilment, a guide to seeing life through a more empowering lens. Each perspective challenges your default thinking and opens up new possibilities, often with just a simple mental shift.

As the author, I've spent years studying human behaviour, psychology, and personal development. My own journey of shifting perspectives has transformed the way I see life, and I've come to realize how powerful a simple change in mindset can be. This book is the culmination of that knowledge, presented in a way that's accessible, engaging, and immediately applicable to your own life.

Each chapter offers a distinct lens, a short powerful mental shift to help you see clearly where you once felt stuck. Collectively, these 16 perspectives form a toolkit for reimagining how you respond to life. And in many cases, they can unlock a calmer mind, better decisions, and greater happiness. The goal is simple: to help you break free from old patterns by thinking differently.

* * *

I

CHAPTER 1: SEEING BEYOND THE MOMENT

This chapter encourages you to step back and gain a broader perspective on life. It emphasizes the importance of looking past immediate circumstances to see the bigger picture, helping you make more informed decisions and align your actions with your long-term goals.

Perspective 1: The Bigger Picture

Welcome to the 1st perspective! It doesn't matter what order you read all the perspectives in, but I'm keeping the perspective at the first place because understanding and keeping the concept introduced here at the back of your mind will help you get a better understanding of the perspectives further.

We humans have reasoning skills, the ability to express emotions, the liberty to act in our ways, and a lot more. We are the most intelligent animals on this planet. And yet, do you think we always behave in our best manner, take the best decisions, and show empathy towards other non-human animals who are incapable of speech and thoughts?

Emotions like anger, sadness, happiness, excitement, jealousy, embarrassment, etc. are part of everyday experiences. These emotions have become so normal that we sometimes don't even notice how much they influence us. Our feelings can become a routine, and we may forget how our emotions affect those around us. Human mind makes us focus more on ourselves, which is why we can sometimes get caught up in our own emotions without realizing their impact on others.

Much of what humans do is driven by the desire to feel good. This idea is known as *hedonism*, the belief that the pursuit of pleasure and the avoidance of pain are central to our decisions. From small daily choices to major life goals, we're often guided by what brings comfort, satisfaction, or joy.

Another explanation from psychology is the *drive reduction theory*. It suggests that we are motivated to act in ways that reduce internal tension caused by unmet needs, like drinking water when we're thirsty or seeking a connection when we feel lonely. In both cases, we're trying to restore balance.

Interestingly, the way we make choices often focuses on quick relief or personal gain, which helps reduce the immediate urge. But this constant need to satisfy drives or chase pleasure can leave us stuck in a loop, never fully at peace, always wanting the next fix.

What if I tell you that there might be a few perspectives to look at life that might can influence and change your thoughts and actions and be able to control your emotions and make more rational decisions in life? In this perspective, we will try to understand different perspectives that might help you look at human beings and life from a different angle. If you share these perspectives too, then according to me, life is simpler than it seems to you.

Humans have an incredible ability to see things from different angles by mentally rotating objects in our minds. This skill is called *mental rotation*. For example, think of a red sports car. First, imagine it from the front, then imagine it from the back. Now imagine it from a side. Were you able to do it? Of course, because according to research, this ability seems to be something we're born with. In fact, studies have shown that even infants can show signs of mental rotation, with this ability developing significantly as they grow, especially between the ages of 3 and 5.

Now, if we can use this ability to look at objects from various angles in our minds, why not apply it to life itself? Just as we can mentally rotate an object to understand it better, we could try to view life from different perspectives. This means stepping back from our usual way of thinking and trying to see situations, challenges, or even people from other viewpoints. It could help us gain a deeper understanding, reduce conflicts, and perhaps even find solutions we might not have seen before. Think of a disagreement you've had with a friend. Instead of only seeing the issue from your side, imagine rotating the situation mentally, just like turning a 3D object. What might it look like from their angle? What were they feeling, assuming, or fearing? By mentally placing yourself in their shoes, you're practicing the same skill we used to rotate objects, only now it's helping you gain emotional clarity and avoid snap judgments. So, if mental rotation helps us understand objects more clearly, maybe using the same approach could help us understand life and the world in a more holistic way.

There are two different viewpoints in this perspective which aim to explain the same thing. Let's start with the first viewpoint. From the first viewpoint, we will try to understand the size of the existence of human beings and what role we share in the entire universe. Have you ever imagined the size of one person in this universe? How do we look if looked at us from outer space? Can you find yourself by looking at the globe? What is the value of human existence from that angle?

Outer-Space Viewpoint

Let's first understand where our planet Earth is in this entire universe. Don't worry, this is not an astronomy class, but knowing some facts would help you think differently. Our sweet planet Earth is a part of the solar system. The solar system comprises eight planets, including Earth, and it's centered on the Sun. Earth is the third planet from the Sun, meaning we are in the middle of the planet's arrangement. One mind-boggling fact is the distance between Earth and Neptune, the outermost planet in our solar system. This distance is a massive 4.5554 billion kilometers. That's how far we are from the furthest planet in our solar system, and we haven't even reached beyond our own system yet! But the solar system we live in is not the only one in the universe. Our solar system is just one of countless others scattered across the vastness of space. There are billions of stars, each possibly having its own set of planets orbiting around it, forming their own solar systems. There are countless other solar systems out there in the universe, each with their own unique characteristics. The universe is far bigger than we can even imagine!

The size of our universe is bigger than you possibly think. But don't worry, I will not point out each and everything about the universe, but it should be enough to get a broader view of our existence. Once we go beyond our solar system, we see the

Milky Way, a galaxy crowded with over 10 billion other planets like ours. From this view, our planet Earth looks like a tiny dot, and don't even ask how humans look from there. If we zoom out even further, there are many more galaxies, planets, stars, solar systems, etc. with massive sizes than we can think.

You would be wondering, why should you know all this? I'm not telling you all this with the purpose of sharing knowledge about astronomy, but to change your perspective on life by showing you the reality of how tiny human beings are when compared with the entire universe. The simple thought here is that the existence of human beings, when looking from the perspective of outer space, is next to NOTHING. We look like little ants on the ground who are doing things like fighting with each other, ruining beautiful relationships, showing egoistic behaviour, living life just for the sake of existing, etc. when looked from a broader perspective. Despite that, we often think and act as if the world exists solely for us, rather than focusing on protecting and supporting each other, and the other non-human animals we share it with. Instead of looking at the bigger picture, we tend to narrow our mindset to what we can see and what is around us. If we think with a broader perspective, I believe, we can achieve avoidance of unnecessary emotions, like ego in a positive relationship.

In the viewpoint above, we understood how less significant human beings are when looked from the broader perspective, whereas in the next viewpoint, we will try to understand a different approach that can be useful to portray better behaviour and empathize with people around us.

Anti-groupism Viewpoint

While the Outer-Space Viewpoint helps us understand how tiny we are in the grand scheme of the universe, the *Anti-Groupism Viewpoint* brings this realization into our daily lives. If we are all just tiny beings in this vast existence, then why do we spend so much energy dividing ourselves into groups, fostering rivalry, and creating unnecessary conflicts?

One powerful way to reduce hatred and promote more kindness and humanity is by shifting how we view ourselves and others. We often categorize people based on income, social status, religion, or nationality. This habit of group division, often unconscious, creates distance. For example, separating high-income people from low-income people fuels a sense of inequality and disconnect. But what if we stopped focusing on these differences and instead saw all humans, and even animals, as part of one big group?

This shift in perspective changes everything. We naturally care more about those we feel are "in our group." If we could view everyone as part of the same team, we'd become more empathetic and supportive, just as we are with people we consider family or close friends.

Let's take a closer look at how this applies in everyday situations.

In a classroom, for instance, focusing on the gap between a class ranker and a student who's failing can easily lead to jealousy, frustration, or discouragement. But if both students saw themselves as part of a shared journey, learning, growing, and striving for a better future, their dynamic would change. They might become sources of support instead of silent rivals. Shifting focus from personal comparison to collective purpose creates a more encouraging environment.

The same applies in the corporate world. Companies often compete aggressively, guarding secrets and chasing market share. But during crises, like a global pandemic, many organizations set aside rivalry to collaborate. They shared resources, exchanged knowledge, and worked together to create solutions for the greater good. This shows that when we look past competition and start seeing humanity as one big group, we unlock collaboration and collective progress.

All of this reinforces one truth: division fuels tension; unity opens the door to empathy and growth. The Anti-Groupism viewpoint encourages us to stop seeing people through the lens of "them" and start recognizing the "we." Whether in classrooms, boardrooms, or communities, we're all aiming for better lives, meaning, and peace. When we align with this common goal, negative emotions like hate and resentment naturally lose power.

And this mindset doesn't apply only to people, it can apply to challenges too. Sometimes a task can feel overwhelming, but shifting perspective helps. If you compare your current challenge to something even harder, it suddenly feels more doable. Like lifting a lighter weight after struggling with a heavier one, you feel your confidence grow. Similarly, by setting your mind on a greater challenge, your current one begins to look smaller, more manageable, and less emotionally draining.

Ultimately, whether we're adjusting how we see people or how we view problems, it's all about perspective. Seeing ourselves as part of a larger, unified group makes us more compassionate and less reactive. It helps us make decisions with empathy, not ego. The more we zoom out, the less power our biases and divisions hold.

Because in the grand scheme of things, we're all just trying to figure life out. And once we see that we're not in competition but in community, everything begins to change.

* * *

Perspective 2: Life vs. the Stock Market

Let's dive into perspective 2! Some ideas seem unrelated until you look a little closer. Life and the stock market, on the surface, belong to different worlds. One is emotional, personal, and unpredictable. The other is numbers, trends, and timing. But when observed with the right lens, their patterns begin to feel familiar. This perspective invites you to slow down and notice that connection. Not to treat life like a market, but to recognize how both follow rhythms we often overlook.

What is the stock market?

At its core, the stock market is a place where ownership of companies is bought and sold. While it often fluctuates based on the basic laws of supply and demand, that is only one part of the picture. In reality, the stock market is influenced by a range of complex factors, including investor sentiment, speculation, macroeconomic trends, government regulations, and even geopolitical events. The law of demand states that the more the demand for a particular stock, the higher the price, and vice versa. But this is not always a rational process. Emotional decisions, media hype, and fear of missing out can create price surges that defy logic. Similarly, as prices rise, more people want to sell that stock because they have already made a profit. Now, with more people willing to sell and fewer willing to buy, demand decreases, leading to a drop in price. This is why stock prices fluctuate. However, this explanation is a simplification. Real-world market movements are often unpredictable and driven by a web of interconnected factors beyond just supply and demand. The more the people, the more the fluctuations, and the fewer the people, the more stability.

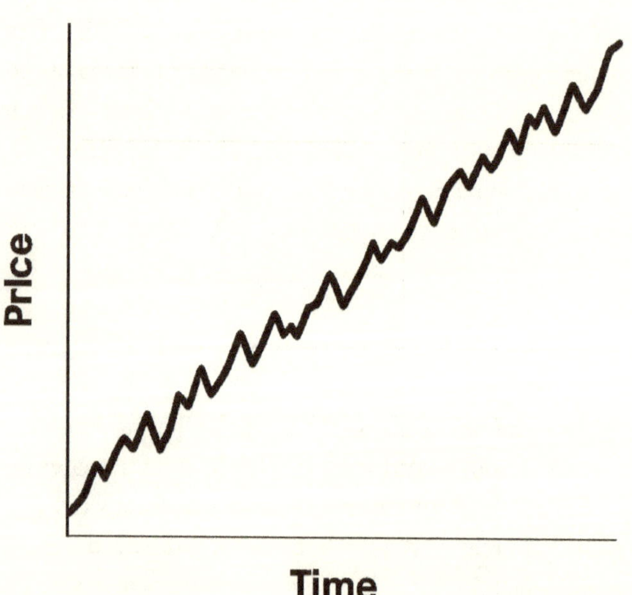

Look at a typical stock price line chart. The line is not straight. It moves up and down, sometimes sharply and other times more slowly. There are moments when it grows quickly, crashes suddenly, or stays flat for a long time before gradually improving. But if you zoom out and look at the bigger picture, you will see that, overall, a strong stock market tends to go up over time despite all the ups and downs.

Comparison with life

Life works in much the same way. Just like a stock market, everyone goes through their own phases of growth and struggle. There are days when everything seems to go perfectly. Your work and personal life are thriving, your confidence is at its peak, and you feel unstoppable, like a stock soaring during a period of major growth. But then, things can shift. You might face setbacks, deal with failures, or experience emotional lows. This is like the market going into a downturn. These tough moments are a natural part of life, just like the bear phase of the market. The key is that, like the market, life tends to move upward in the long run, even though the journey can be unpredictable.

Some people panic during downturns, just like investors who sell off their stocks out of fear. Others remain patient, understanding that downturns are temporary and that consistency, resilience, and smart decisions eventually lead to recovery and growth.

Short-term volatility vs. long-term growth

Short-term volatility in investing refers to the daily ups and downs of the market, which can often trigger emotional responses from investors. Those who fixate on these fluctuations may panic when prices drop and make impulsive decisions, such as selling their assets at a loss. However, experienced investors understand that markets are inherently unpredictable in the short term but tend to grow over the long run. Instead of reacting to every minor dip, they remain patient, stick to their strategy, and focus on the bigger picture. This disciplined approach allows them to benefit from long-term growth, compounding returns, and overall wealth creation.

The same principle applies to life. Temporary setbacks, failures, and disappointments can feel overwhelming in the moment, but they are just part of a larger journey. If you judge your progress solely based on short-term difficulties, you may become discouraged and give up too soon. However, success often requires perseverance through challenges. Just like markets recover from downturns, personal growth comes from learning through adversity. Those who stay focused on their long-term vision, rather than getting discouraged by temporary struggles, are the ones who ultimately achieve their goals.

In both investing and life, resilience is key. Instead of making decisions based on emotions triggered by short-term volatility, one must develop the patience and confidence to stay the course. By keeping a long-term perspective, you can navigate uncertainties without losing sight of your ultimate goals.

Diversification in life

Diversification is a fundamental principle in investing. A wise investor spreads their money across multiple stocks rather than relying on a single stock or industry. This strategy minimizes risk because if one investment underperforms, others may balance out the losses, ensuring financial stability. A well-diversified portfolio provides protection against volatility and increases the chances of long-term growth.

In investing terms, this means not letting one company or even one sector define your financial outcome. Similarly, in life, you cannot let one area define your entire identity or happiness. If you invest all your energy into just one area, whether it is career, relationships, finances, or health, you make yourself vulnerable. For example, if someone is solely focused on their career but neglects their health, a sudden illness could derail everything they have worked for. Similarly, if a person's entire happiness depends on one relationship, its failure could leave them emotionally shattered.

Just like investors mitigate risk by diversifying, you create emotional and personal stability by balancing your time, effort, and identity across different areas. Building strong relationships, maintaining physical and mental health, pursuing financial security, and nurturing personal growth all contribute to overall well-being. That way, when one area faces difficulties, the others provide a safety net, preventing a complete collapse.

A good life portfolio, just like a good investment portfolio, ensures that no single failure can ruin your overall progress.

Emotional investing vs. emotional living

In investing, emotions can be a major obstacle to success. Many investors fall into the trap of buying when the market is soaring because they feel optimistic, and selling when it crashes out of fear. This emotional cycle leads to poor decision-making. Buying high and selling low becomes the pattern, rather than following a strategic and long-term approach. Successful investors recognize that markets move in cycles, and they train themselves to stay rational despite short-term volatility. They do not let emotions dictate their actions. Instead, they rely on research, patience, and a clear investment strategy.

Now apply this to your daily life. Emotional living is like emotional investing. It may feel right in the moment, but it often leads to irrational decisions that you regret later. If you let excitement, fear, anger, or disappointment control your actions, you might make decisions that are not in your best interest. For example, making big life changes out of frustration, responding harshly in relationships due to momentary anger, or giving up on a goal because of temporary setbacks can all lead to unnecessary struggles. Emotional reactions in life can cloud judgment and lead to instability.

Just as an investor builds emotional discipline to avoid market panic, you need emotional awareness to avoid impulsive living. Instead of reacting impulsively, learn to step back, observe your emotions, and make decisions based on logic and long-term goals. Developing self-awareness, practicing patience, and maintaining perspective can help you navigate both financial markets and life's ups and downs with confidence.

Both investors and individuals who master their emotions are the ones who stay grounded, make wiser choices, and see consistent progress over time.

The power of compounding

Compounding is one of the most powerful forces in investing. When you invest money, the returns generated do not just sit idle. They get reinvested and begin earning additional returns. Over time, this snowball effect leads to exponential growth, where even small, consistent contributions can result in significant wealth. The key to compounding is patience and consistency. Those who start early and stay committed see the greatest benefits.

This principle applies far beyond investing. In life, every productive action, no matter how small, builds on itself when repeated regularly. Personal growth is not about making one big leap. It is about the small, consistent efforts that add up over time. Learning something new each day, staying disciplined in your work, nurturing relationships, and taking care of your health might not seem transformative in the moment, but their effects compound over years. A person who reads daily, even for just 15 minutes, accumulates vast knowledge over a decade. Someone who exercises regularly builds lifelong health and energy. Just like reinvested profits generate more profits, daily habits create a ripple effect that enhances every area of your life.

However, much like in financial markets, negative habits also compound. Ignoring health, avoiding learning, or neglecting relationships may not show immediate consequences, but over time, they lead to major setbacks. This is why being intentional about what you invest your time and effort into is crucial.

Think of each choice you make, how you spend your time, what you focus on, and the habits you build as a deposit into your personal growth portfolio. Whether in wealth-building or personal development, the power of compounding is a reminder that small, consistent actions are far more impactful than occasional bursts of effort. Success is not about instant results. It is about staying committed to steady growth over the long run.

If you zoom in on a stock market chart, you will see unpredictable movements, spikes, and crashes that make it look chaotic. But if you zoom out and look at the long-term trend, the market generally moves upward.

Life is the same. If you judge your progress based on a bad day, week, or even year, it may seem like you are failing. But when you look at the bigger picture, you will see growth. The key is to stay invested, ride out the lows, and trust that in the long run, everything moves forward.

* * *

II

CHAPTER 2: THE UNNOTICED EXCHANGES IN LIFE

Here, we explore the subtle, often overlooked exchanges that shape our lives. By recognizing these hidden interactions, you can better understand the dynamics that influence your actions, relationships, and overall well-being, leading to more conscious and intentional choices.

Perspective 3: Life's Double-Entry System

Congratulations, you've successfully explored the first two perspectives! And I believe this is great progress because it takes a good amount of mental energy to try to change your viewpoints regarding things. Reaching this point means you're showing mental resilience and growth. It's a sign that you're capable of adapting and learning, which is a huge strength. Changing your viewpoints isn't just about accepting new ideas; it's about being open to seeing the world differently, which helps you grow as a person.

Now let's jump to the 3rd perspective, the double-entry system of life. Perspectives 3 and 4 are both from the financial world, and that's why they are positioned together. If you're familiar with the financial accounting concepts, then you must be aware of the double-entry system. But if you're unaware of it, I'm going to explain it here. Don't worry, I'll try not to use numbers as much as possible, I promise! As you already know, in the 1st perspective, we took an astronomical approach to look and understand life; now we're using accounting to do the same. The idea of using the concepts we already understand to make sense of new things is a powerful way to expand our perspectives. Our brains are wired to make connections between different ideas, which helps us learn and adapt more easily.

When we compare life to something we're already familiar with, like a theory, a concept, or even the way our body works, we can break down complex or abstract concepts into something more relatable and easier to grasp. It's like using a map to navigate a new place. We already know how maps work, so when we apply that knowledge to a new situation, it makes it simpler to understand and process. The more we practice linking new ideas with things we already know, the more flexible and open-minded we become. It's a way to constantly expand our thinking and gain new insights.

Before understanding the double-entry system of accounting, it's important to start with the basics. Honestly, I'm not an expert in accounting too, but when I got to know the concepts, I immediately compared them with life and how we can make our lives happier using these concepts.

In accounting, the double-entry system ensures that every transaction affects at least two accounts—one is debited and the other credited—so that the accounting equation (Assets = Liabilities + Equity) always stays balanced.

For instance, when a company buys a machine with cash, it increases (debits) the machine account while decreasing (credits) the cash account. Nothing is created or lost, just transformed. The total financial picture remains in equilibrium.

Debit and credit

Most of us have come across the terms debit and credit, especially when looking at bank or credit card statements, and these concepts are actually quite central to how our finances work. But if you're not entirely sure about how they work, no worries, I'll explain them in a simple way.

What is debit? A debit is when money is taken out of your account. It means you're spending money or reducing your balance. For example, when you make a purchase using your debit card, the money comes directly from your checking or savings account. So, think of it this way: when you debit something, it's like you're "paying" or "withdrawing" money from your account. In a bank statement, it would show up as a debit because your account balance is decreasing.

Now, what is credit? A credit, on the other hand, is when money is added to your account. It means you're either receiving money or your balance is going up. For example, if you deposit money into your account or if your paycheck is direct-deposited, that's a credit. In simple terms, debit means money out and credit means money in.

Alright, now that you have a grasp on the concepts of debit and credit, let's jump to the double-entry system in accounting. I understand that you might be wondering, 'What do these accounting ideas have to do with understanding life?' Well, stick with me, and I'll clear up that confusion for you in no time. You'll soon see how these principles can provide a powerful lens through which to view the complexities of life.

Double-entry system

Now let's understand the double-entry system. In simple terms, double-entry accounting is a method used by accountants to keep track of a business's financial transactions. It is based on the principle that every transaction has two sides: a debit and a credit. So, for every amount that's debited to one account, another amount is credited to a different account, and vice versa. In other words, for every debit transaction that takes place in one account, there has to be a credit transaction in another account so that it always balances.

This system helps prevent errors and ensures transparency. The logic is that value doesn't disappear, it just moves. That's the essence of balance. Imagine you borrow $1000 from a friend. When the friend gives you the money, they transfer it directly into your bank account. So, when you check your bank statement, you'll see a deposit or "credit" of $1000. This means the friend has added that amount to your account. At the same time, the same $1000 is removed from your friend's account. In other words, they give you the money by taking it from their resources, and in your account, it shows up as a credit of $1000. One account's entry is credit and the other account's entry is debit, and both are balanced out: double-entry system.

Let's understand this concept with another example. To make it less complicated, imagine that the total amount of money in the world is $100, and the total population of the world is 5 people: A, B, C, D, and E. Out of those 5 people, only "A" has all the money ($100). Now imagine that person "A" decided to give each person $20. What would happen to the total amount of money between all the 5 people? Nothing, right? This transaction does not create or destroy money—it simply transfers a portion of the total wealth from one person to another. The total amount is still $100, no new wealth has been generated; it has only been redistributed. The transaction can be seen as a simple shift where A's balance is debited by $80, and B, C, D, and E's balances are credited by $20 each.

	Bank balance before	Bank balance after
A	$100	$20
B	$0	$20
C	$0	$20
D	$0	$20
E	$0	$20
Total	$100	$100

The table above illustrates that the total amount of money remains the same; the only thing that is happening is money changing hands. That means it is balanced.

Now that we've understood the basic concept of the double-entry system of accounting, along with debit and credit, let's apply that same idea to our lives, specifically, to understand how we can make life happier.

Comparison with life

Just like in accounting, where every transaction has both a debit (something that is given) and a credit (something that is received), we can look at life through a similar lens. The goal here is to understand that just as the amount of $100 didn't change, but just got distributed to different people. Similarly, resources in this world are limited; they just get distributed to different people.

Think of your actions and choices as entries in your personal life ledger. When you give effort to a goal, it's a debit from your comfort or leisure, but a credit toward growth, discipline, or future results. And just like in accounting, if you only debit and never credit, or vice versa, your life becomes unbalanced. Talking about time and efforts, let's take an example of that. Just as discussed above, time and effort are also finite resources. When you put time and energy into learning a skill, you are debiting your time and energy from one area of life and crediting it toward personal growth. For example, a student sacrifices social outings to prepare for exams. The hours spent studying are debited from leisure time and credited into their knowledge bank. Let's take another example: a person waking up early to go to the gym is making a similar transaction. Sleep, comfort, and short-term laziness are sacrificed, and physical fitness, discipline, and long-term health are gained.

Emotions, like money, flow between people and experiences. When you give happiness to others, you are debiting from your emotional reserve but crediting it into someone else's life, and often, it comes back to you in unexpected ways. Imagine a person paying for a stranger's coffee at a café, only a small amount of money is debited in their account, but they managed to credit happiness in the other person's life.

The same effect can happen with negative emotions too. Imagine a manager under stress yelling at an employee. He debited anger from his life, but credited frustration in the employee's life. The transaction can have chain effects as well. Imagine that employee carries their frustration home and yells at their son. And their son starts crying. In this situation, they debited frustration from their life but credited sadness in their son's life.

Let's take an example with a non-living thing. When mining companies mine gold from the underground, they gain (or credit) gold, but that gold is reduced (or debited) from the Earth.

In some cases, debit and credit transactions can take place twice in a single situation. For example, knowledge. Imagine a professor giving a classroom presentation to their students. They share knowledge, but that knowledge is not debited because knowledge is one of those few resources that can't be debited when shared. So what's debiting here? Mental efforts! They are using a structured mental effort in order to pass their knowledge in an orderly manner that can be understood by the students. On the other hand, students are also crediting knowledge but debiting mental efforts, because the knowledge that the professor is sharing needs an attentive mind to understand. Similarly, to read and understand this book, you're debiting resources like time, money, and mental effort, but you're crediting an understanding of new perspectives. That's how life mirrors the double-entry principle: every investment you make, even if it costs you something, adds value elsewhere.

The best approach in life would be to balance all the resources in your life. Take this as a positive attitude: your loss is not an actual loss, it's just transferred and you've gained something with it. Life is about managing your resources wisely, whether it's money, time, effort, or emotions. Spend, invest, and distribute them in ways that create value for yourself and others. By mastering this mindset, we stop fearing losses. And as I said in the first perspective, keeping the big picture in mind will help in the perspectives ahead. Similarly, start seeing the bigger picture of life's debit and credit transactions.

* * *

Perspective 4: The Win-Win Strategy

This perspective is a bit different from the ones we've explored so far. Until now, we've examined perspectives that compare life to various external systems. But now, let's shift our focus inward, toward something that governs much of our personal and professional lives: groups. We'll explore how to succeed in any group and, potentially, become the group leader. Whether it's a workplace team, a social circle, or even a family unit, groups function based on complex dynamics.

Understanding Group Dynamics: The Power of Every Individual

Think about a sports team. The idea of teamwork is crucial, but the team's overall success is really a reflection of how well each individual player performs. This same concept applies to any group. What does that mean exactly? It means that every person in the group plays a role. Even if someone isn't directly contributing to achieving the group's goal, they still matter because they add something else to the dynamic. For example, they might help brainstorm ideas, coordinate tasks, or act as a bridge between the group and higher authorities.

Even if someone isn't doing any of these things, just by being there, they are still contributing by increasing the group's size. More people in the group can mean more strength, especially in situations where majority decisions are important. In those cases, even the person who isn't contributing much is still valuable because they help create the majority vote.

Now that we understand how everyone in a group plays an important part, let's dive into how we can use this understanding to succeed in a group and possibly even become the leader. Imagine there are 10 people in the group, including yourself. This means each person holds about 10% of the group's influence (10 people × 10% = 100%). Below is a tabular representation of this calculation.

Members	Percentage
Member 1	10%
Member 2	10%
Member 3	10%
Member 4	10%
Member 5	10%
Member 6	10%
Member 7	10%
Member 8	10%
Member 9	10%
Member 10	10%
TOTAL =	**100%**

From this, we understand that each member has some level of influence in the group. To succeed in a group, we need 100% of the members to be agreeable to us. Even if one member is against us, there's a high chance we won't be able to win the whole group over because that member may have already started changing others' minds or creating internal conflicts, like groupism. That's why we need every member (all 100%, including yourself, obviously) to be in favor of you.

The Win-Win Strategy: A Two-Layered Approach

Now, how do you make this happen? This is where the concept of the "Win-Win Strategy" comes in. It's different from the usual "win-win situation," where two sides benefit equally. In this case, the first "win" is about you winning individually, and the second "win" is about winning over the entire group. In simpler terms, the "Win-Win Strategy" means that, in order to succeed in a group, you need to make sure every single person in the group is on your side.

To win the support of the entire 10-member group, it's crucial to win over each individual 10% to make the total 100%. How do you do that? The key is to build personal connections with each member. Since you're already part of the group, you automatically have your own 10%. Now, you need to win the remaining 90%, which means you must win over the other 9 members. You can achieve this by getting to know each person in the group and forming genuine friendships. People are more likely to support you when they feel like you understand and care about them as individuals. When you understand what motivates each person, what they care about, and what they're struggling with, you're able to align your actions with their needs. This makes your presence feel valuable to them. People tend to follow those who make them feel seen and heard. Leadership, then, doesn't come from telling others what to do—it comes from becoming someone who supports, empowers, and elevates others. When individuals in the group feel that you care about their individual success, they begin to trust your judgment and willingly support your decisions. Staying in touch with them, even when the group isn't meeting, shows that you value the relationship beyond just working together. Showing care, paying attention to their needs, concerns, and goals makes them more likely to reciprocate and trust you.

By putting effort into networking and building personal relationships with each member, you'll gain their trust and support. Each 10% will become part of your influence, helping you to ultimately win over the entire group. Of course, group dynamics in real life are more complex than simply getting everyone to like you. People come with different personalities, values, and levels of influence. Some may naturally resist your efforts, while others might have stronger voices within the group due to their experience, confidence, or existing relationships. Power dynamics, unspoken alliances, and hidden conflicts can all play a role. That's why the Win-Win Strategy isn't about pleasing everyone or forcing unity—it's about building enough trust and credibility so that even when disagreements arise, your voice is still respected. The goal isn't perfection—it's creating an environment where people feel heard and where your presence consistently adds value to the group.

If you manage to win over all 9 other members in the group, there's a good chance you'll start learning personal things about them. For example, imagine you're on a college project team. You make an effort to learn what each person is good at, help them when they're stuck, and give credit when they contribute something valuable. Over time, people start turning to you—not just because you're competent, but because you're the one who makes them feel respected and understood. Slowly, without realizing it, the group starts seeing you as the one who "keeps things together," and when a decision needs to be made, they look to you for direction. When you're all together as a group, each person might feel like you're a close friend who knows their personal stories and understands them better than anyone else. This makes you stand out and gives you a special place in the group.

As a result, people will naturally start to feel more comfortable around you. You might notice them talking to you more often, choosing to walk beside you, or simply hanging out with you because they trust you. These small, subtle actions are important because they show that people are genuinely at ease with you, and that's a powerful sign in group dynamics.

When everyone in the group sees that you have positive relationships with everyone, they'll begin to see you as a central figure, someone everyone respects and feels comfortable with. The more people feel this way about you, the more likely they are to follow your lead. They'll listen to your opinions, value your feedback, and agree with your judgments. Before you know it, you'll have become the 'untold leader' of the group, someone everyone naturally turns to for guidance and decisions, even though no one has officially given you the title of leader.

These dynamics create a sense of unity and trust, and as the group's natural leader, you'll have the ability to influence the group's direction and decisions without needing to assert power directly.

Reducing Negative Emotions

Another major benefit of this strategy is that it helps reduce negative emotions like jealousy and resentment, which can often arise in group settings. When you take the time to connect with everyone and build trust, you create a positive environment. This can lead to people feeling more comfortable and supported, making it less likely for negative emotions to take hold. In fact, the more you work on forming these strong, genuine relationships, the more you increase the chances of creating an overall positive vibe within the group.

Even if the other members start talking among themselves and realize you're close friends with everyone, there's no need to worry. In fact, this is a good thing! It shows that you've worked hard to build relationships and trust with every member of the group. People will notice that you've made an effort to connect with everyone, and they'll respect that. Rather than causing any problems, it will only boost your influence in the group, as people will admire your ability to get along with everyone and build a united, supportive atmosphere.

In short, by forming these strong bonds with everyone, you not only strengthen your position within the group but also create a more harmonious environment, where negative feelings like jealousy are minimized. This positive dynamic will naturally make people more inclined to listen to you and support you in group decisions.

Mastering the Win-Win Strategy is not just about gaining influence; it's about becoming the person people naturally gravitate toward. The ability to connect with every individual in a group is a skill that sets leaders apart from followers. Think about the most charismatic and influential people you've ever met. Were they the loudest? The most dominant? Probably not. Instead, they were the ones who made everyone feel valued, the ones who could walk into any room and instantly create a sense of trust and belonging. They listened more than they spoke. They noticed the small things others missed. That presence made people feel seen, heard, and understood. That is the real power of winning in a group, not by force, not by authority, but by becoming someone people want to follow.

When you implement this strategy, something incredible happens: you no longer have to chase opportunities; they come to you. People start seeking your advice, your approval, your presence. Whether it's in a workplace, a social setting, or even within your family, you become the glue that holds everything together. Decisions start revolving around you, discussions feel incomplete without your input, and even when you're silent, your presence is felt.

The most beautiful part? This influence doesn't come at the cost of others; it elevates everyone. When you focus on building genuine relationships rather than competing for dominance, you create an environment where everyone wins, where you thrive, the group thrives, and together, you achieve far more than any individual ever could alone.

This is what makes the Win-Win Strategy so powerful: it transforms influence into a natural result of empathy and connection, rather than a goal you have to chase. And now, with this new perspective, the question is: how can you apply this to your own life? Think about the groups you are part of right now. Is there a way to shift your approach? Can you strengthen your connections, deepen your influence, and become the person people naturally look up to?

* * *

III

CHAPTER 3: THE WAY WE JUDGE AND MEASURE OTHERS

In this chapter, we dive into how judgments are formed and the biases that influence our perceptions of others. By understanding these judgments, you can develop a more empathetic and accurate view of the people around you, which can improve your interactions and relationships.

Perspective 5: The First Judgement

We all know about evolution. It suggests that living organisms change gradually over many generations, evolving from earlier forms into new species. For example, humans are believed to have evolved from apes. But obviously, during that time, we were not intelligent enough to create society and civilization. As humans developed intelligence, we also created complex mental frameworks that shape our interactions.

Now, we live in a world shaped by human-made systems, things like culture, religion, social structures such as castes, and the use of currency to exchange goods and services. These systems weren't always there, but they developed as humans grew more advanced. Perspective is something we create in our minds through a combination of sensory information, past knowledge, experiences, and personal motives. Everyone's view of the world is different, largely because people have different experiences and purposes in life. For instance, someone who is colorblind might see the world very differently from someone who isn't. Even the personalities of our parents or the way we were raised can play a role in shaping how we see things. This is why no two people see the world in exactly the same way. Ultimately, our individual perspectives are a combination of the information we take in, our life experiences, and the motivations we have. Since everyone's life journey is different, each person's view of the world will naturally be different too.

As humans, we live in a civilized community, and despite our differences, we also share many things in common. One of those shared experiences is the idea of first judgment, or in other words, how people judge someone when they meet for the first time. The concept of first judgment refers to the way people tend to evaluate others based on certain predetermined criteria in their minds, assuming the population is generally normal and reasonable. But what exactly influences these quick judgments?

In my view, there are two basic criteria by which people form first impressions. This does not refer to people who already know each other but to those initial impressions created when meeting someone new. Of course, the human mind and thoughts are far more complex than what we will explore here, but understanding this can help reveal one important aspect of life. Human behaviour is triggered by both the conscious and the unconscious mind, and it is important to understand that these early judgments can happen on either level.

The two basic criteria are physical traits and mental traits. People also form impressions based on things like body language, communication style, and overall presence. These subtle cues often shape how trustworthy, confident, or competent someone appears. However, in most situations, the first judgment is largely influenced by physical appearance and surface-level mental traits. These act as shortcuts for the brain, especially during brief interactions.

Physical Traits

One of the two criteria by which people tend to make the first judgment is physical traits. Physical traits include everything related to physical appearance. Obviously, there are many physical characteristics of a human body that can be used to describe a person, but the two most important traits are how good a person looks and how rich a person looks.

Let's start with one of the two physical traits. When people see someone for the first time, their first impression is often based on looks. They don't necessarily need to have a conversation or get to know the person to decide if they find them attractive. In fact, this judgment can happen even from a distance, just by observing how someone appears from afar. Some people might claim that they don't judge others based on their looks, but in reality, this judgment often happens on an unconscious level. They may not even realize that they tend to give more attention or favor to those who are considered good-looking. It is something that happens automatically, without them being fully aware of it.

Why do people favor good-looking individuals? In my opinion, the answer to this question is very interesting. Good-looking people often get more attention, which can lead to more opportunities, a larger social circle, and even a more active romantic life. For example, imagine two job applicants walk into an interview. One is conventionally attractive, well-groomed, and confident. The other is equally qualified but appears less polished. Research suggests that the first candidate might unconsciously be perceived as more competent, even if both have the same skills. This preference for attractiveness is not always fair, but it highlights how appearance plays a role in first impressions. These advantages contribute to a higher sense of confidence and make them feel more special or valued. This boost in confidence, in turn, helps them develop stronger social skills. When someone feels good about themselves, they tend to engage with others more positively, which makes them even more attractive to people around them. This creates a kind of positive feedback loop, where their appearance leads to more success, and that success boosts their social abilities, which then draws in even more people.

In simple terms, it is like a cycle. Good looks lead to more confidence and social success, and that success makes them even more appealing to others. This cycle keeps repeating itself, strengthening the advantage they already have.

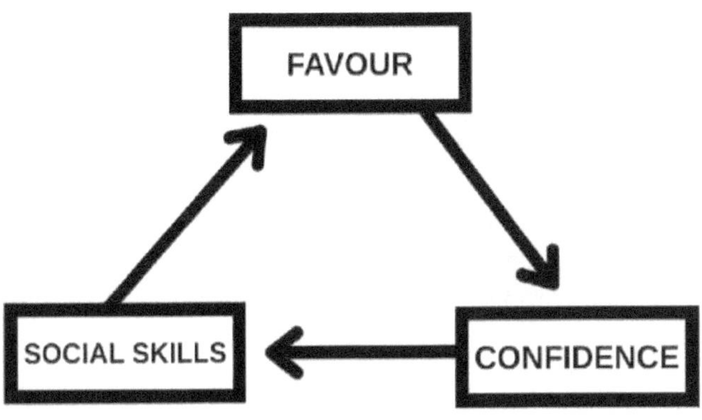

Of course, life and human behaviour are much more complex than just this cycle of attraction and confidence. There are many other factors at play, such as jealousy, competition, and even biases, which can sometimes create tension or negative emotions. People may feel threatened by others who seem to have an advantage, and that can lead to things like resentment or hatred. However, it is important to try to understand these patterns, even if they are not always perfect or fully explain everything. Recognizing how these patterns work can help us create a more balanced and empathetic society where people are not judged solely based on their looks.

Another way people often judge others at first glance is by how wealthy or well-off they appear. This is another physical trait that can influence how people are perceived. In today's world, first impressions also take place online. In this age of social media, appearances can be deceiving. Someone dressed in designer brands might be perceived as wealthy, even if they are deep in debt. This is because humans tend to associate luxury items with success, a concept known as material signaling. But in reality, financial stability is not always reflected in outward appearance. Looking rich does not mean being rich. There are two possibilities. First, the person actually has a good amount of money and is rich. Second, the person only looks rich. These two possibilities are independent of each other. People who look rich may or may not actually have money, and vice versa.

Once, when I was at a business event, I noticed a man walk in wearing a simple shirt, worn-out shoes, and no flashy accessories. He stood alone, scrolling through his phone, not making much eye contact. A group nearby whispered, "He doesn't look like someone important." Then, during the panel discussion, this same man was introduced as the keynote speaker, a self-made entrepreneur who had built three successful companies. The moment he started speaking, the room went silent. His clarity, depth of thought, and calm confidence shifted everyone's perception. It was a reminder that most people form their first judgments based on how rich or attractive someone looks. But more often than not, those snap judgments are blind to someone's true substance.

People who appear wealthy often receive more favors than others. This happens because, whether consciously or unconsciously, others believe that helping rich people might lead to financial benefits for themselves. They think that by helping wealthy individuals, they might learn ways to make more money or gain access to valuable resources. Even subtle interactions with affluent people are seen as opportunities for personal gain. Additionally, people assume that rich individuals are connected to other successful people, like business owners or politicians, so they try to get close to them, hoping it could open doors for them too. They believe that proximity to wealth increases their own chances of success.

Mental Traits

As mentioned earlier, the second criterion by which people make their first judgment is mental traits. Just like physical traits, mental traits include many things, but we will focus on only one: knowledge or education.

Knowledge and education have some obvious differences, but in my opinion, education is the proof of attainment of knowledge. Even if a person completed their education credentials just for the sake of passing rather than gaining deep knowledge, there would still be a difference in perspective between educated and uneducated individuals, as education encourages critical thinking. Please note that by education, I mean a credential that is earned, not bought. While formal education is often seen as proof of expertise, it is important to recognize that knowledge can also be gained through experience. Entrepreneurs, artists, and innovators sometimes achieve mastery without traditional degrees.

Now you may be wondering how first impressions are affected by someone being educated. More education usually means more knowledge, and more knowledge means expertise in a particular area. For example, we trust doctors because they have spent many years studying medicine, making them experts in the field. If we only knew someone was a doctor, we might begin believing everything they say about health and medicine. This idea is not limited to doctors. Anyone with a lot of education or knowledge becomes an authority in their field. Take a person with a PhD, for example. Their education proves their expertise, and because of this, they can become a professor and teach others. The knowledge they have places them in a position of authority.

Humans tend to trust people in these authoritative positions, which can sometimes lead us to be influenced by their opinions more than we realize. This is known as authority bias, a psychological tendency where we are more likely to believe what an authority figure tells us simply because of their position or title.

First impressions are natural, shaped by both physical and mental traits. Whether we realize it or not, we often favor those who appear attractive, wealthy, or knowledgeable. But what if we looked beyond the surface and gave people a chance to reveal who they really are? Instead of making quick assumptions, we could develop the habit of seeing people with curiosity rather than judgment. Because in the end, the depth of a person is not always visible at first glance.

* * *

Perspective 6: The Human Rating Formula

Welcome to the 6th perspective!   In the last perspective, *The First Judgment*, we explored how people form first impressions and judge others at first glance. We discussed the factors that influence these snap judgments and how physical and mental traits play a significant role in shaping perceptions. Now, in this perspective, we take it a step further. Instead of just understanding how people judge one another, we will learn how to rate a person's overall standing in life—whether they are below average, average, or above average. To do this, we will use three primary factors: education, personality, and wealth.

However, it's important to recognize that this approach is a simplified framework that reflects common societal patterns. It is not an absolute measure of human worth or complexity.

So, how do we determine where someone stands? We simply rate each factor out of 10 based on the criteria provided in this perspective. By summing up these scores, we get an overall rating that helps assess a person's level in life. Let's get started.

Education

Education has long been considered a status symbol in society. The higher the level of education, the more respect and authority a person tends to receive. Educated individuals are often viewed as more knowledgeable, competent, and deserving of leadership roles. In Perspective #2, we linked education with knowledge. However, in this perspective, we will treat education and knowledge separately. Here, education will be considered purely as a rating indicator, while knowledge will be discussed under personality.

For instance, a doctor or professor is often perceived as more authoritative compared to a self-taught entrepreneur, even if the entrepreneur is financially more successful. This is because education carries an inherent credibility factor, making people naturally inclined to trust those with formal qualifications.

Let's take a look at the criteria by which we can rate a person out of 10. Below is the rating scale influenced by general societal perception:

- No education or below high school diploma – **0 points**
- High school diploma – **2 points**
- Bachelor's degree (e.g., BA, BBA) – **5 points**
- Master's degree (e.g., MA, MBA) or professional degree (doctor, engineer, chartered accountant) – **8 points**
- Doctorate (e.g., PhD, DBA) – **10 points**

The points increase with higher levels of education, allowing us to assess a person's educational standing in life. However, education alone does not determine a person's overall rating. To get a complete picture, we must also consider personality and financial standing, which play equally important roles in the final evaluation.

Personality

While education provides credibility, personality is what truly defines a person's presence and influence. A well-educated individual might command respect, but if their personality is weak, they may not be taken seriously beyond their credentials. Personality encompasses a wide range of traits, including:

- Confidence – How self-assured and assertive a person is in conversations and decisions
- Communication Skills – The ability to articulate thoughts clearly and persuasively
- Emotional Intelligence – Understanding and managing emotions effectively, both in oneself and in interactions with others
- Adaptability – The ability to handle different situations and challenges with ease
- Knowledge and Awareness – Education and knowledge often go hand in hand, but unlike education, which is about formal qualifications, knowledge is about real-world understanding and intelligence. A person can be highly knowledgeable without having a degree
- Physical Appearance and Grooming – While natural looks are not in one's control, how a person presents themselves is. Dressing well, maintaining good hygiene, and having

a neat appearance can impact first impressions and how others perceive one's personality

Below is the rating based on how society generally views individuals in terms of personality:

- Poor social skills, negative, unapproachable – **0 points**
- Low confidence, struggles in conversations – **2 points**
- Average social skills, decent communication – **5 points**
- Confident, well-spoken, approachable – **8 points**
- Charismatic, inspiring, highly influential – **10 points**

Based on this table, rating a person's personality will help us determine their overall score in the final calculation.

Wealth or Financial Standing

Now that we've covered education and personality, let's move to the final and perhaps the most universally recognized factor: wealth. While education provides credibility and personality shapes influence, money is often seen as one of the most important measures of success in society. Financial status plays a significant role in how people are perceived and treated by others. Money creates an undeniable advantage in life:

- Respect and Influence – People naturally pay more attention to those who are financially successful. Their opinions are valued, and their presence is acknowledged.
- Opportunities and Network – Money provides access to better opportunities, high-profile connections, and an influential social circle.
- Confidence and Freedom – Financial security allows a person to make independent choices and live life on their own terms.

Despite being one of the most important things in the world, money alone is not enough to rate a person. Someone with wealth but a weak personality or lack of education might not be truly respected. They may be feared or envied but not necessarily admired. For example, a middle-class individual with strong personality traits and knowledge might earn more respect in social circles than a billionaire who is rude and lacks social skills.

Here's a simple rating scale for wealth or financial standing:

- Struggling with basic needs – **0 points**
- Financially stable but limited or no savings – **2 points**
- Comfortable with steady income and savings – **5 points**
- Wealthy with multiple income sources – **8 points**
- Financially independent and highly successful – **10 points**

Now that we have assigned ratings for education, personality, and financial standing, we can move forward with the final calculation. By summing up these three scores, we can determine a person's overall rating in life.

The Human Rating Formula

The formula is simple. Add the scores of education, personality, and wealth. Based on that total, we can evaluate how society might perceive a person's overall position in life, not their actual worth.

Total Score = Education Score + Personality Score + Wealth Score

Since each factor is rated out of 10, the maximum possible score is 30. Based on the total score achieved, we can categorize people into three broad levels:

- Below Average (0–14 points) – Individuals in this range may lack financial stability, struggle with social interactions, or have limited education. They often find it difficult to gain respect or influence in society
- Average (15 points exactly) – A score of 15 suggests a balance among the three factors, meaning the individual is neither significantly ahead nor behind the general population
- Above Average (16–30 points) – Individuals in this range excel in at least one or more factors, making them more successful, respected, and influential

Let's take a look at how this formula applies to different types of people, such as celebrities. Celebrities often score high in personality and wealth, which significantly boosts their overall standing. Their visibility and social influence further amplify the impact of these factors, making them appear even more admirable or successful in the eyes of society.

For example, let's analyze a typical successful celebrity:

- Personality: 8/10 – They are charismatic, well-spoken, and have strong social skills
- Wealth: 8/10 – They have multiple income sources, endorsements, and financial stability
- Education: 5/10 – Some celebrities hold a bachelor's degree or higher, while others may not have formal education but rely on their talent and network

Total Score: 8 (personality) + 8 (wealth) + 5 (education) = 21

Since their score is above 15, they are clearly in the "Above Average" category. In fact, most well-known figures, whether in entertainment, business, politics, or sports, score above 15 because they have mastered at least two of the three critical factors.

However, it's important to emphasize that this formula is not a definitive or complete evaluation of a human being. It simplifies the complexity of life into three measurable categories. While useful for understanding societal patterns, it should never be mistaken for a measure of someone's inner value, contribution to the world, or true potential. People are far more nuanced than any framework can capture. Every individual carries experiences, emotions, and intentions that numbers cannot quantify, and those elements shape the essence of who they are.

The Human Rating Formula is not meant to judge people in a rigid way, but rather to provide an objective lens through which we can understand how society perceives success and influence. While some may score lower in one area, they can compensate by excelling in another. This perspective helps us understand why certain individuals gain more respect, authority, and admiration than others.

Alternative ways of assessing personal growth, such as values, resilience, emotional depth, and societal impact, are equally important and cannot be captured by numerical ratings.

Remember that this is just a personal observation, not an absolute rule. Society has certain patterns in how it perceives success, and this formula simply reflects those general trends. It is not a measure of a person's actual worth or potential. Someone with a low score today could completely change their trajectory with the right mindset and actions. At the end of the day, life is not about fitting into a formula. It is about growth, self-improvement, and defining success on your own terms.

So, while this perspective offers a unique way to analyze how people are commonly perceived, it should be used with care, humility, and awareness of its limitations. True success and fulfillment go beyond numbers; they are deeply personal, multi-dimensional, and ever-evolving.

* * *

IV

CHAPTER 4: THE HIDDEN PATTERNS OF COMMUNICATION

Communication is more than just words. This chapter uncovers the unspoken patterns and nuances in how we express ourselves and interpret others. Mastering these patterns can enhance your ability to connect with people and communicate more effectively.

Perspective 7: The Positive-Negative-Positive Approach

Have you ever been in a situation where you needed to say "no," but didn't know how to do it without hurting someone's feelings? Saying "no" is tough for many people. Whether it's turning down an invitation, refusing to help with something, or giving someone feedback, we often get stuck in the moment. We might worry about damaging a relationship or upsetting the person on the other end. The fear of confrontation, guilt, and worry about their reaction can make us want to avoid saying "no" altogether. But the problem with avoiding these conversations is that it can lead to stress, frustration, or the feeling of being overwhelmed. Over time, it can even build resentment.

What if there was a way to communicate difficult messages without leaving a negative impression? A way to decline requests, give feedback, or set boundaries while still maintaining warmth and positivity? This is where the Positive-Negative-Positive approach comes in.

This approach is a structured way of handling such situations with grace and tact. It allows you to communicate your boundaries while preserving a positive relationship with the other person. The method involves three steps: start with a positive remark, deliver the difficult or negative message in the middle, and end on a positive note. This structure softens the impact of the message and helps ensure that the conversation ends on good terms. The other person doesn't feel completely rejected or disheartened.

This technique is based on cognitive psychology, which shows that people tend to remember the first and last things they hear more than the middle. So, when you start and end on a positive note, it can soften the effect of the more difficult message in between. Think of it like a sandwich: the two slices of bread represent the positive parts, while the filling in the middle is the tough message. When used correctly, this approach can make uncomfortable conversations smoother and more productive. Instead of leaving someone feeling dejected, they walk away with a more balanced perspective.

Imagine a situation where a friend invites you to an event, but you're not interested or simply don't have the time. Instead of outright saying, "I can't come," which may sound abrupt or dismissive, you can use the Positive-Negative-Positive approach to deliver the message more effectively.

First, start with a positive statement. Begin the conversation with something appreciative or complimentary. This helps the person feel valued and sets a positive tone. For example, you could say, "Hey, I saw the pictures from your last event, and it looked amazing! You always bring such great energy to these gatherings." Even a small compliment can go a long way in softening the conversation. It shows you're paying attention and genuinely care about the person you're speaking to, which builds trust and makes it easier to address sensitive topics if needed. Starting with positivity opens the door to a more productive and respectful exchange.

Second, deliver the negative message—the "no"—by communicating the difficult part clearly and respectfully. For instance, "I really wish I could make it this time, but my schedule is completely packed, and I won't be able to join." The message is direct but not harsh.

Finally, end on a positive note. Conclude the conversation with something reassuring or forward-looking. This ensures that the relationship remains intact. You could say, "But let's definitely catch up soon. I'd love to hear all about it! Maybe we can plan something for next weekend?"

This approach doesn't change the fact that you are saying no, but it makes the other person feel respected and valued. It reduces the chances of them taking it personally.

The reason this method is effective is psychological. People tend to focus more on the beginning and end of interactions than the middle. By starting and ending with positivity, the difficult message feels less harsh. Studies in communication and negotiation show that how you say something is often more important than what you say. A poorly delivered "no" can harm relationships, while a well-structured one can actually strengthen mutual respect. This highlights the power of framing in communication. It can transform potentially negative conversations into opportunities for growth and understanding

Another reason this approach works is that it acknowledges the other person's emotions. Most of the time, people just want to feel heard and appreciated. By recognizing their effort or value before saying no, you prevent them from feeling dismissed. Ending with something positive also reassures them that your "no" is not a rejection of them personally, it's simply a limitation in the given situation.

Let's understand this with a few real-life scenarios.

Imagine your colleague asks you to take on an extra project, but you're already overloaded with work. Instead of bluntly refusing, you could say:

"You always bring such great ideas to the team, and I really appreciate how you're driving this project forward. Right now, my plate is completely full, and I wouldn't be able to give this the attention it deserves. But I'd love to support in smaller ways. Maybe I can review your final draft or help brainstorm ideas?"

By responding this way, you avoid coming across as unhelpful while still setting a clear boundary.

Now consider a more personal situation. Saying no to friends and family can be even harder because of emotional ties and the fear of damaging close relationships. Suppose your sibling asks for financial help, but you're not in a position to lend money. A direct "no" might hurt them, but a Positive-Negative-Positive approach could look like this:

"I know how hardworking you are, and I admire your dedication. Right now, I'm managing my own expenses carefully, so I won't be able to lend money at the moment. But if you need any advice on managing finances or exploring other options, I'd be happy to help."

This way, you maintain your boundary while also showing care and support.

Now imagine needing to give negative feedback without demotivating someone. This approach is especially useful. For instance, if a friend asks for feedback on their speech but it needs improvement, you could say:

"I really love how confident you sounded, and your energy was great. One thing that could make it even better is slowing down a bit so the message comes across more clearly. But overall, I think you're doing an amazing job, and I can't wait to see how you refine it further."

They are more likely to take your advice positively rather than feel criticized.

Now, let's explore how to implement this in daily life. First, practice framing conversations in your head before responding to a difficult situation. Take a moment to structure your response using this approach. As you continue through this book, you'll see how exposure plays a crucial role in making this process second nature. The more you practice framing your responses intentionally, the more natural and effortless it will become. This idea of gradual adaptation through repeated exposure will be explored further in Perspective #13, The Power of Exposure.

Second, observe how people respond when you use this method. Are they more receptive? Less defensive? This feedback will help you refine your approach.

Lastly, apply it consistently. Whether in emails, texts, or face-to-face conversations, consistent use will make it a natural part of how you communicate.

Saying no doesn't have to be uncomfortable or damaging to relationships. The Positive-Negative-Positive approach provides a framework to navigate difficult conversations in a way that is clear, respectful, and relationship-friendly. This technique is not about sugarcoating the truth but about delivering it effectively. Whether in professional settings, friendships, or personal relationships, this approach can help you communicate your boundaries without guilt while maintaining strong connections.

In the end, how we say something is just as important as what we say. Mastering the art of difficult conversations through structured communication can make us more confident and effective in all areas of life.

* * *

Perspective 8: Reflective Behaviour

In the previous perspective, we explored how to deliver a negative message without hurting someone. We focused on our approach, choosing the right words, tone, and structure to ensure the message is well-received. However, communication is a two-way street. No matter how carefully we frame our words, the way the other person perceives and interprets the message depends on their mindset, experiences, and emotional state. This perspective shifts the focus from how we deliver a message to how the other person receives it. Instead of viewing communication solely from our lens, we now put ourselves in the recipient's shoes and analyze the filters and biases that influence their interpretation.

Human behaviour is often seen as a reflection of personal values, upbringing, and character. But what if behaviour is more fluid than we think? What if how someone acts toward us is not entirely their own choice, but a response influenced by our actions and characteristics? This is where the concept of Reflective behaviour comes into play.

Reflective behaviour suggests that when people meet for the first time, they begin with a neutral stance, neither positive nor negative. However, their behaviour quickly adapts based on the interaction. This doesn't mean they simply mirror or imitate the other person. Rather, they have pre-recorded behavioural responses in their minds to certain types of people. Their reactions are shaped by past experiences, beliefs, and subconscious patterns. Even so, people's neutral stances vary. For example, an aggressive person may have a more assertive or dominant baseline behaviour, while someone naturally calm may appear more passive or reserved. This means that even before interaction shapes their response, their baseline demeanor is already influenced by their personality traits and past conditioning.

Consider a person with a curious mind. Their reaction will vary depending on whom they meet. If they encounter someone knowledgeable and insightful, they'll naturally show excitement, engagement, and positivity. If they meet someone who lacks intellectual curiosity or knowledge, they may become disinterested and distant. This is not a conscious decision but an automatic response driven by internal expectations and previous experiences.

At its core, Reflective behaviour revolves around commonness. The more similarities two individuals share, the more likely they are to have a positive interaction. Conversely, the fewer commonalities they have, the higher the chances of disinterest, avoidance, or even negative behaviour. This perspective provides a practical way to understand social dynamics and predict how people will react to one another in different situations. It emphasizes how shared traits such as values, habits, or experiences can silently shape the energy of any conversation. Even subtle overlaps in personality or worldview can create a sense of ease and familiarity, often without either person realizing why.

While human behaviour is shaped by a range of factors such as emotions, personality, and context, this perspective emphasizes commonness as a key driver of Reflective behaviour. In many cases, people's responses are not as unpredictable as they seem. Much of their reaction is a conditioned pattern shaped by past interactions and familiarity, rather than a purely spontaneous or random choice.

This idea of commonness applies to all social interactions. Let's take some examples. An extroverted, outgoing person may act highly engaged with another outgoing individual but seem quieter or uninterested when interacting with an introvert. A person who is highly competitive in sports may enjoy talking to another athlete but feel indifferent toward someone with no interest in sports. These responses happen instinctively, based on what their subconscious has learned from previous interactions. Imagine a person who loves reading books meeting another book lover. They will naturally engage in deep conversation, share recommendations, and feel an instant connection. On the other hand, if a book lover meets someone who only plays video games and has no interest in literature, the conversation might feel forced, short-lived, or even awkward.

Commonness also applies to lifestyle choices, professions, and worldviews. A highly disciplined person may find it frustrating to talk to someone who lacks self-control, while a business-minded individual may feel more drawn to others who share an entrepreneurial spirit. The level of commonness acts as a guide, influencing whether the interaction will be pleasant, neutral, or negative. Now that we've understood Reflective behaviour, let's explore how we can apply it to improve our social interactions.

Predicting Reactions

One of the key benefits of understanding Reflective behaviour is the ability to predict how people will react in different situations. Since behaviour is often a response rather than an independent action, recognizing this pattern allows us to anticipate and adjust our approach accordingly. For example, if someone values direct communication, we can present our message clearly rather than using vague or indirect language. If we're dealing with someone sensitive to criticism, we can adopt a more encouraging tone to ensure they receive our feedback constructively. By being aware of pre-recorded behavioural responses, we gain better control over social interactions, reduce misunderstandings, and increase the likelihood of a positive outcome. Instead of assuming people act randomly, we begin to see patterns, allowing us to navigate conversations with greater confidence and effectiveness.

Enhancing Connections

At the heart of every strong relationship, whether personal or professional, is a sense of connection. Understanding Reflective behaviour helps us foster this connection by recognizing that people naturally gravitate toward those who share common interests, values, and ways of thinking. When we actively seek common ground, we create a comfortable and familiar environment that encourages meaningful interaction. For example, in a networking setting, if we identify shared experiences or mutual interests with someone, the conversation will naturally flow better, leading to a stronger bond. On the other hand, if we ignore commonalities and focus only on differences, the interaction may feel forced or awkward. By being aware of this, we can strategically align our communication to build rapport and make interactions smoother and more enjoyable. Recognizing that people respond positively to familiarity allows us to create deeper connections effortlessly.

Reducing Misinterpretations

A common source of conflict in social interactions is misinterpretation, when one person's words or actions are perceived in a way that was not intended. Reflective behaviour helps us minimize this by shifting our perspective from self-centered thinking to an understanding of behavioural conditioning. Instead of immediately feeling offended or hurt by someone's reaction, we can take a step back and consider whether their response is simply a pre-programmed behaviour rather than a personal attack. For example, if someone reacts negatively to constructive criticism, it might not be because they dislike us but because they've developed a defensive mechanism due to past experiences. By recognizing this, we can avoid unnecessary conflicts and misunderstandings. This perspective also helps us become more empathetic, as we begin to see that people's reactions are often shaped by their history rather than being a direct reflection of our actions.

Improving Influence

One of the most powerful applications of Reflective behaviour is its ability to enhance influence and persuasion. When we understand that people's reactions are driven by their internal behavioural patterns, we can adapt our communication style to align with their subconscious responses, making our message more effective. For instance, if we are trying to persuade someone who values logic and facts, presenting a well-reasoned argument with evidence will yield better results than relying on emotional appeals. Conversely, if we are dealing with someone who is emotionally driven, focusing on storytelling and personal experiences may be more impactful. This concept is especially valuable in leadership, sales, and personal relationships, where the ability to influence others effectively plays a crucial role in success. By tailoring our approach based on how people naturally respond, we can increase our impact, gain trust, and improve our ability to communicate persuasively.

Reflective behaviour challenges the idea that people act independently of external influences. Instead, it suggests that behaviour is highly dependent on past experiences, the person they are interacting with, and the level of commonness they share. This understanding can help us navigate social interactions more effectively by focusing on areas of commonality rather than differences.

By recognizing and applying Reflective behaviour, we can become more socially intelligent, predict reactions better, and create smoother, more meaningful interactions. Instead of seeing social dynamics as random or unpredictable, we can approach them with a strategic mindset, understanding that people don't just act but react based on their internal programming.

* * *

V

CHAPTER 5: HOW TO MEASURE REAL PROGRESS

True progress is often misunderstood. This chapter guides you on how to evaluate your growth in a more meaningful way, beyond conventional markers of success. By understanding the true nature of progress, you can stay focused on what truly matters to you.

Perspective 9: The Scale of Realization

Let's explore perspective 9! Life is in a constant state of change, whether we actively pursue growth or remain stagnant. Even when we feel like we're standing still, time moves forward, and subtle shifts take place within and around us. This chapter explores how to recognize, measure, and appreciate progress, both visible and unseen, so you can gain a deeper understanding of your personal growth journey.

Life is often described as a journey, but what we sometimes fail to acknowledge is that our experience of this journey is shaped by the way we measure our progress. Are we moving forward fast enough? Are we ahead of others or falling behind? These questions can make us anxious, leading us to constantly compare ourselves to those around us. But what if there were a more balanced, grounded way to assess where we stand in life, one that reduces anxiety rather than fuels it?

Imagine standing on a long staircase, with countless steps behind you and many more ahead. At any given moment, you have two choices: you can look down to see how far you've come, or you can look up to see where you're headed. Both perspectives shape how you view your journey, yet many people focus on just one, either feeling content with past achievements or endlessly chasing the next milestone.

This balance between reflection and ambition is what I call *The Scale of Realization*, a mental framework that helps us evaluate our position in life. When we look down, we acknowledge our progress, recognize the privileges we often take for granted, and cultivate gratitude for what we already have. Looking up, on the other hand, allows us to set new goals, visualize the future, and stay motivated to grow. Both perspectives are essential, but if we lean too far in one direction, we risk either complacency or constant dissatisfaction. In this chapter, we'll explore how to maintain this balance and use *The Scale of Realization* to navigate life's ever-evolving journey.

Striking a balance between these two perspectives is the key to living a fulfilling life. If we only look down, we risk stagnation. If we only look up, we might never feel satisfied. *The Scale of Realization* provides a structured way to find clarity by helping us appreciate the present while remaining ambitious about the future. Understanding this mental model and learning how to apply it regularly can lead to a more intentional, stable, and fulfilling life.

Let's revisit the staircase example to understand this perspective better. Imagine standing in the middle of a long staircase. The steps below represent people who have less than you, who may not have had the same opportunities, privileges, or circumstances. The steps above represent those who have achieved more, who have set higher targets and worked toward greater accomplishments. *The Scale of Realization* is this very staircase, where you stand in the middle, constantly aware of both sides.

Looking down helps you recognize your privileges. Maybe you have access to education, a supportive family, or financial stability, things that many people struggle to attain. This perspective fosters gratitude, reducing unnecessary dissatisfaction. It's a powerful reminder that, no matter how challenging your situation may seem, there are always people who would consider your life a dream. This awareness is crucial in preventing entitlement and keeping you grounded.

At the same time, looking up is equally important. If you only focus on those who have less, you might become complacent, believing you have already achieved enough. Looking up allows you to set meaningful goals and push yourself toward growth. It provides inspiration and motivation, showing you what's possible. It's not about comparison for the sake of feeling inadequate; it's about using others' success as a roadmap for your own ambitions.

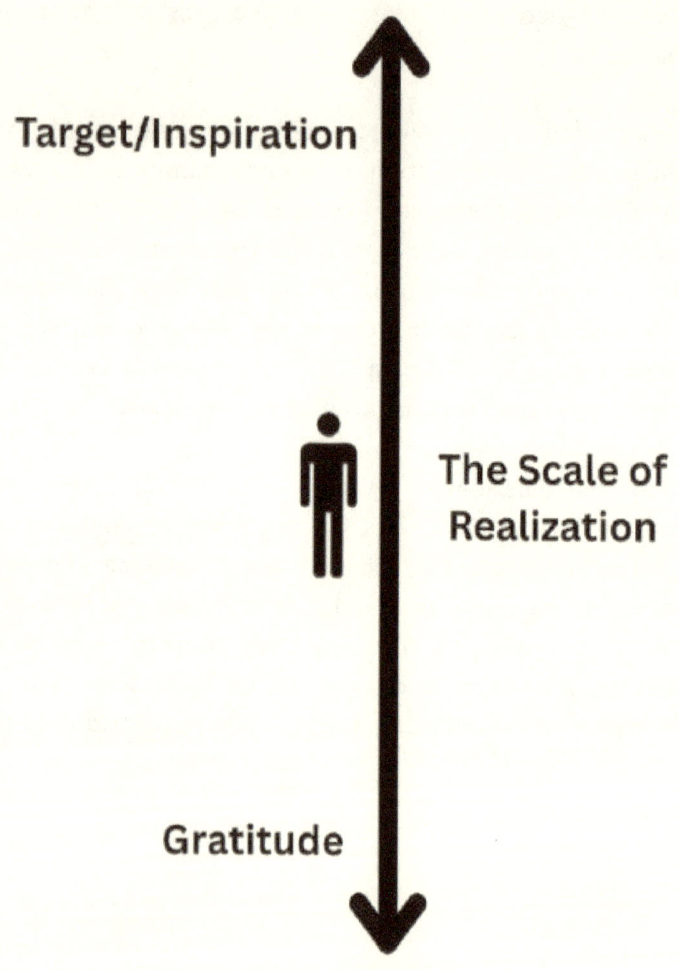

One of the biggest mistakes people make is getting trapped in just one perspective. Those who only look down may feel grateful but fail to set higher goals, limiting their potential. They might convince themselves that since they are better off than many, there is no need to strive for more. This mindset can lead to complacency and cause them to miss out on opportunities for growth and self-improvement.

On the other hand, those who only look up may become overwhelmed by the pressure of constant ambition. The endless pursuit of success can make them feel like they are always behind, leading to dissatisfaction, stress, and even burnout. An excessive focus on upward comparison can also create entitlement or arrogance. When people only measure themselves against those ahead, they might believe success defines their worth, leading to strained relationships and an unhealthy mindset.

A well-balanced approach is to use *The Scale of Realization* as a dynamic tool, regularly shifting between looking down to appreciate what you have and looking up to redefine where you want to go. The middle position is not about stagnation; it's about maintaining awareness of both perspectives. By staying grounded in the center, you can live with gratitude without complacency and pursue ambition without anxiety.

Morning Gratitude, Evening Ambition

How you start and end your day shapes your mindset. Begin each morning by looking down, acknowledge the things you're grateful for, whether it's your health, past achievements, or simple everyday comforts. This sets a positive tone and reminds you of how far you've come.

At night, shift your focus upward. Reflect on where you want to go, what goals need your attention, and how you can improve.

This daily cycle of gratitude and goal-setting creates a healthy rhythm between contentment and motivation.

Compare with Purpose

Comparison is natural, but it can either uplift or destroy your mindset. When you catch yourself comparing to others, ask: Am I using this comparison to feel grateful or to set a goal? If the comparison makes you feel inferior, pause and shift your focus to gratitude. If it inspires you to improve, let it drive you forward. The key is to ensure that comparison serves a constructive purpose, not a destructive one.

Journaling the Two Perspectives

Writing down your thoughts strengthens your mindset. Keep a dedicated journal where you record: One thing you appreciate about your life (looking down) and one goal you are working toward (looking up). This simple habit keeps both perspectives in check. Over time, you'll see clear evidence of your progress while staying motivated for the future.

Avoid Extremes

Many people unknowingly lean too far in one direction. If you find yourself too content, you may be avoiding growth. If you're constantly unsatisfied, you might be neglecting gratitude. It's easy to fall into a rhythm without realizing it's leading you off track. That's why reflection isn't a luxury; it's a necessity. Whenever you catch yourself stuck in either extreme, pause and recalibrate. If you've been overly focused on achievements, take a moment to appreciate what you already have. If you've been too comfortable, challenge yourself with new goals. Self-awareness is key to maintaining balance.

Teach the Scale to Others

One of the best ways to reinforce this mindset is to share it. When you see someone complaining about life, remind them to look down and appreciate how far they've come. When someone seems too lazy, encourage them to look up, set goals, and work toward them.

Discussing this concept with friends, family, or colleagues not only helps them but also strengthens your own understanding. The more you teach, the deeper it integrates into your own belief system. By applying these simple techniques, *The Scale of Realization* becomes more than just a theory; it becomes a guiding principle for how you live your life.

Life is not a race, nor is it a static experience. It's a continuous movement between gratitude and ambition. *The Scale of Realization* provides a simple yet powerful way to navigate this journey with clarity and balance. The key is to stay in the middle, not to be consumed by either extreme. If we only look down, we might miss out on our full potential. If we only look up, we might never feel satisfied. But when we embrace both perspectives, we create a life that is both fulfilling and progressive.

So, the next time you feel lost in comparison, unsure of where you stand in life, take a moment to visualize the *Scale of*

Realization. Look down and appreciate your journey. Then, look up and decide where you want to go next. In this balance, you will find both peace and purpose.

* * *

Perspective 10: Change as a Sign of Progress

L et's move on to the 10th perspective! Progress is always happening, but how do we recognize it? This perspective highlights change as one of the signs of progress. While progress isn't always visible, change serves as an indication that something is shifting, whether in our mindset, habits, or circumstances.

Change is unsettling. It disrupts the familiar, challenges our comfort zones, and forces us to adapt. Most people resist change because it comes with uncertainty, effort, and discomfort. Whether it's switching careers, moving to a new city, ending relationships, or even changing daily habits, there's always a part of us that wonders if the change is worth it.

This resistance is natural. The human brain is wired to seek stability because stability feels safe. Change, on the other hand, triggers fear, fear of failure, fear of making the wrong choice, and fear of losing what we currently have. Many people spend their lives avoiding change, hoping to find progress while staying within their familiar routines. But here's the paradox: progress and change are inseparable.

If we want to grow, evolve, and become better versions of ourselves, change is not just an occasional inconvenience; it is proof that we are progressing. A life that looks the same year after year is not a sign of stability; it's a sign of stagnation. If everything about your life, your thoughts, habits, relationships, career, and emotions remain the same for years, can you truly say you have progressed? The evidence of personal and professional growth lies in the changes we undergo.

In this perspective, we'll explore why change is one of the most reliable proofs of progress, why not all change is necessarily positive, and how to assess whether the changes we experience are leading us in the right direction.

Progress is often misunderstood. Many people measure it by achievements, status, or wealth. But progress is not always visible in external accomplishments. True progress happens when our mindset, behaviours, and approach to life evolve. Change is what signifies that evolution.

Imagine a person who, for years, has struggled with social anxiety. They avoid gatherings, keep conversations brief, and prefer to stay in their comfort zone. Now, imagine that over time, they start attending social events, engaging in conversations, and even initiating meetups. These changes, though subtle at first, are undeniable signs of progress. Each small step reflects a shift in their mindset and behaviour. Even if they haven't become the most confident person in the room yet, the fact that their behaviour has changed means they have grown.

Similarly, think about someone who is learning a new skill, say, playing an instrument. In the beginning, their hands fumble, the notes sound off, and progress seems slow. But as time passes, their muscle memory improves, they can play songs more smoothly, and their confidence increases. The fact that their skill level changed and is now different from where they started is the proof that they are progressing.

One of the most profound examples of change as progress is in our mindset. Let's say someone has always believed that failure is a sign of incompetence. This belief has held them back from taking risks, trying new things, or pursuing ambitious goals. Over time, after reading, learning, and experiencing life, they begin to see failure differently, not as an endpoint but as a stepping stone to success. They start taking calculated risks and embracing challenges. This shift in perspective is one of the most valuable forms of progress, and it is only evident through change.

People often fail to recognize their own progress because they are looking for big, dramatic milestones. People should keep the bigger picture at the back of their mind, but when setting goals, they should keep small targets because real progress is reflected in the small changes: how you think, how you react to situations, how you handle emotions, and how you approach problems. Even if your career position hasn't changed in a year, if your mindset towards work has shifted and your skills have improved, that is still progress. Small, consistent improvements accumulate over time, often leading to more significant changes than we initially realize

A practical way to track your progress is to look back at your past self. Compare your thoughts, decisions, and habits from a few years ago to where you are now. Have your perspectives changed? Have your habits improved? Do you handle situations differently? If the answer is yes, that is proof that you are evolving.

But let's also acknowledge an important distinction: not all change leads to growth. Some changes can represent setbacks, regress, or stagnation, especially if they stem from stress, avoidance, or negative coping mechanisms. For instance, a person might stop engaging with others, skip workouts, or give up on personal goals, not because they are at peace, but because they feel overwhelmed or defeated. These are changes, but they don't point to progress.

The Absence of Change Creates the Illusion of No Progress

Progress is constant; our work, mindset, skills, and relationships are all progressing, but change acts as proof of that progress. At the same time, the absence of visible change can make us feel like nothing is happening. Let's understand this with an example: Imagine two cars driving side by side at the same speed on a highway. Since their relative positions remain unchanged, the drivers might feel as if they're not moving at all, almost like they're parked. In reality, they are moving, but without noticeable change, the motion becomes an illusion of stillness. This example shows how the absence of noticeable change can make progress feel nonexistent, while even a small shift can distort our perception of movement.

It's easy to fear change, but it's harder to deny its importance. Every significant achievement in life, whether personal growth, career advancement, or relationship improvements, comes from embracing change. Growth is not always comfortable, but it is always rewarding. The same principle applies to emotional growth. Someone who used to react with anger or frustration in difficult situations might gradually learn to respond with patience and understanding. Their ability to remain calm in stressful situations is a clear indicator of progress, even if it happens gradually.

Change as a Sign of Regress

Change is undeniably a sign of progress, but it can also indicate regression. When we see movement, whether in our personal lives, careers, or society, it often suggests that something is evolving. Learning new skills, adopting better habits, or experiencing shifts in mindset are all forms of change that signify growth. Even small adjustments, like refining our routines or gaining new perspectives, contribute to forward momentum.

However, not all change is beneficial. Just as improvement requires change, so does decline. Losing discipline, adopting negative habits, or falling into unproductive cycles are also changes, just in the wrong direction. A business experiencing rapid changes in leadership might be progressing, or it could be falling apart. A person who shifts their mindset may be evolving, or they might be losing sight of their values.

Change can also create the illusion of regression, even when no actual regression is happening. Imagine someone scrolling through social media and seeing their peers land promotions, travel, or hit milestones. Even though they're making quiet, steady progress, learning, building habits, or healing, it might feel like they're falling behind. But in reality, they're not regressing; it's just someone else's movement creating a false sense of being stuck or going backward. This illusion can distort our perception of our own path. This shows that change, while real, doesn't always mean decline; sometimes, it's just a shift in perception.

This dual nature of change is why it's important to evaluate movement carefully. Is the change bringing you closer to your goals, or further away from them? While positive change leads to growth, learning, and improvement, negative change can result in setbacks and decline. However, it's also important to recognize that not all perceived regress is real. Sometimes, change can create an illusion of moving backward when, in reality, no actual loss has occurred.

The key is to evaluate change carefully. Instead of assuming all movement is progress or all setbacks are failures, we should assess whether a change is bringing us closer to our goals or pulling us away. Recognizing this distinction helps ensure that change becomes a tool for true progress, not an illusion of it.

Ask yourself today: What has changed in me over the past year? What new habits have I developed? How have my thoughts evolved? The answers to these questions will show you how much progress you've truly made. Change is not the enemy; it is the proof that you are on the right path. And when it's not, it's a signal that something needs reflection and realignment. Either way, it's worth paying attention to.

* * *

VI

CHAPTER 6: MASTERING YOUR EMOTIONS

Emotional mastery is key to living a balanced life. In this chapter, you'll learn how to navigate your emotions, understand their impact, and use them as a tool for better decision-making and personal growth.

Perspective 11: The Reality of Emotions

Let's begin with the 11th perspective! This perspective dives deep into understanding emotions from a fresh perspective. Emotions are a powerful force in our lives. They shape our decisions, influence our relationships, and impact our overall well-being. Yet many people feel controlled by their emotions rather than in control of them. In this perspective, we'll explore how emotions shape our reality, why they often mislead us, and how recognizing their true nature can help us gain better control over our lives.

Imagine you're scrolling through social media. A photo catches your eye. Its colors are vibrant, the lighting is just right, and every detail seems flawless. It looks perfect, almost too perfect. You pause for a moment, knowing that what you're seeing isn't entirely real. The image has been filtered, adjusted, and enhanced to appear more striking than it originally was. Without those edits, the same picture would look ordinary—muted tones, natural imperfections, nothing exaggerated. In this digital age, what we see is often far from what was actually there. The art of manipulation has become a key part of what we accept as beauty.

Now, consider how we experience life. Our emotions act in much the same way. They are like filters that shape the way we perceive the world, amplifying certain moments while dulling others. A small setback can feel like a disaster, just as a fleeting moment of joy can seem like the peak of happiness. Emotions add intensity, drama, and meaning to our experiences, making them feel larger than life. But if we strip away those emotional filters, what remains? A neutral reality. Things simply happening, without exaggeration, without distortion, just as they are.

When we feel anger, it feels like the world has done something unfair to us. When we feel embarrassment, it seems like everyone is judging us. When we feel happiness, life appears brighter and full of possibilities. But in reality, life itself remains unchanged. The events are simply unfolding, and we are the ones adding emotions to them, just like adding a filter to a picture.

Understanding this concept can be life-changing. If we realize that emotions are not the absolute truth but merely an added layer to reality, we gain the power to manage our reactions better. Instead of getting lost in feelings of frustration, sadness, or fear, we can step back and remind ourselves: this is just a filter. Without it, everything is simply neutral.

How Emotions Distort Reality

To truly understand the illusion of emotions, let's break it down. Imagine two people stuck in traffic. One is furious, honking aggressively, feeling that the universe is against them. The other is calm, listening to music, accepting that traffic is just part of life. The situation is the same, but their emotional filters are different. One has applied the frustration filter, making the experience feel unbearable. The other has chosen not to add any strong emotional reaction, making the experience neutral. This is how emotions work. They make things seem bigger than they are. Let's take a deeper look at some of the common emotional filters.

The Anger Filter

Imagine a situation where someone cuts you off in traffic. Instantly, frustration surges through you. How dare they? Do they think they own the road? Your mind starts spinning a story, one where you're the victim of someone else's selfishness or incompetence. This is the anger filter at work, making the event feel like a personal attack rather than a random occurrence.

But if we step back and remove this filter, the situation changes. The other driver may have been in a hurry, distracted, or simply unaware. There was no grand conspiracy against you, just a momentary lapse in judgment. Something that happens all the time to everyone. Without the anger filter, the event remains what it truly is: a simple inconvenience, nothing more. Instead of fueling frustration, you can focus on what actually matters.

The Embarrassment Filter

Think about a time when you made a social mistake. Maybe you stumbled over your words in a conversation, waved at someone who wasn't waving at you, or made a joke that fell flat. In that moment, it felt like the whole world was watching, silently judging you. Your face burned with embarrassment, and you replayed the scene in your head over and over. This is the embarrassment filter in action, making a small, forgettable moment feel like a monumental failure.

But what happens when we remove this filter? We realize that most people either didn't notice or forgot about it within seconds. Everyone is too occupied with their own thoughts, concerns, and insecurities to dwell on our minor missteps. The event wasn't as significant as our emotions made it seem.

Additionally, there are ways to handle embarrassment and other negative emotions more effectively. We will explore one such strategy in the next perspective of this chapter, *The Group Exit Analogy*, which provides a practical approach to moving past these uncomfortable moments.

The Fear Filter

Fear is one of the most powerful emotional filters, often transforming uncertainty into overwhelming dread. It makes unfamiliar situations seem dangerous, exaggerates risks, and convinces us that the worst-case scenario is not only possible but likely. Imagine standing at the edge of an opportunity, whether it's speaking in public, starting a new venture, or making an important decision. Fear whispers: what if you fail? What if people laugh at you? What if you're not good enough?

But what if we strip away this filter? We would see that most of our fears are just thoughts, not real threats. The speech is just a collection of words. The new venture is just a series of steps. The decision is just a choice, one of many we make throughout life. The reality itself remains unchanged. It is only our perception that makes it feel daunting. When we remove the fear filter, we stop seeing everything as a potential disaster and start seeing it as just another part of life's unfolding journey.

The Happiness Filter

Not all emotional filters create negative distortions. Happiness can also act as a filter. One that brightens our view of the world, making everything seem lighter, easier, and more enjoyable. When we are happy, problems seem smaller, people appear friendlier, and life feels effortless. We might even overlook flaws or ignore warning signs simply because our mood is so elevated.

While this isn't necessarily a bad thing, it's still an illusion. The moment the happiness filter fades, whether due to stress, fatigue, or an unexpected setback, our perspective shifts. What once seemed perfect now appears flawed, and reality feels harsher in contrast. Understanding this filter helps us appreciate happiness while staying grounded in reality. True contentment comes not from ignoring life's imperfections but from accepting them, knowing that neither good nor bad moments define the bigger picture.

The key to emotional intelligence is recognizing that these filters are not reality. They are temporary distortions created by our minds. This understanding doesn't mean we should suppress emotions, but rather see them for what they are: temporary, subjective, and often misleading.

Now that we understand emotions as filters, how can we use this knowledge in daily life? The answer lies in awareness. Whenever you feel overwhelmed by an emotion, pause and ask yourself: what filter am I using right now? How would this situation look without this emotional layer? Is my reaction based on reality or just my perception? Let's look at some practical examples.

Imagine you have to give a speech, and you feel intense fear. Your mind tells you: everyone is watching. If I mess up, they'll think I'm a failure. But if you remove the fear filter, what's actually happening? People are just sitting there. They are not analyzing every word. Some might be busy munching. And they will probably forget your mistakes within minutes. The fear is an illusion. It's just a filter distorting reality.

Let's see another example. A friend doesn't reply to your message for hours. The frustration filter tells you: they're ignoring me. They don't care about me. But if you remove the filter and look at reality, the truth is simple. They might just be busy. It's not a personal attack. Without emotions, it's just a message waiting for a reply.

Now imagine you apply for a job and don't get selected. The disappointment filter makes you feel like a failure. But what's the reality? A company made a decision based on their needs. It's not about you as a person. Without the emotion, it's just an event. Nothing more.

This mindset shift can make life much easier. Instead of getting caught up in emotions, we can step back and view life as it is. Neutral. Unfolding naturally. Without the dramatic layers we often add. Emotions are not reality. They are just the lens through which we experience it. While this perspective presents emotions as filters that influence how we see reality, it is important to acknowledge that emotions are not just distortions. They are also essential to human experience. Emotions play a vital role in motivation, decision making, and social connection. The filter metaphor is a simplified way to understand how emotions can shift our perception, but it is not the complete picture of their purpose. If we learn to recognize when we're looking at life through a filter, we gain immense power over our thoughts, reactions, and overall well-being. Instead of being controlled by emotions, we can observe them, manage them, and navigate life with clarity. So next time you feel overwhelmed, remind yourself: this is just a filter. Without it, everything is simply happening.

* * *

Perspective 12: The Group Exit Analogy

Welcome to perspective 12! This perspective is all about reducing negative emotions by shifting the way you see and respond to them. Often, we get stuck in emotional loops, feeling overwhelmed by embarrassment, frustration, disappointment, or stress. But what if managing negative emotions wasn't about fighting them, but about changing your approach?

Think about the last time you felt embarrassed. Maybe you said something awkward in a conversation, tripped in public, or made a mistake at work. In that moment, it probably felt like the world was watching, judging, and remembering your every move. The embarrassment felt intense, almost unbearable, as if that moment would be etched in everyone's memory forever.

Now, take a step back. Can you remember the last time someone made an embarrassing mistake in front of you? Maybe a friend tripped, someone misspoke in a meeting, or a stranger spilled coffee on themselves. Chances are, you don't remember many of these moments, and if you do, it's likely a vague memory without much emotional weight.

This raises an important realization. While we hold onto our own embarrassing or negative experiences, others rarely do. People are too busy thinking about their own lives to dwell on our awkward moments. In fact, most negative experiences fade into irrelevance unless we choose to keep them alive in our minds.

Now, consider a simple analogy. Imagine a WhatsApp group where people once actively messaged. Over time, one by one, everyone exits. Finally, the last person leaves. What happens after that? The group ceases to exist. It's gone. Not archived. Not hidden. Completely erased. It's like the group never even existed.

Of course, emotions aren't as simple as exiting a chat. Emotional healing involves time, reflection, and sometimes support. But this analogy isn't meant to oversimplify. It's meant to remind us of something empowering. We have a choice. A choice to stay engaged with thoughts that hurt us, or to mentally step away from them.

Negative emotions work the same way. We are the last person in that group keeping it alive. Negative emotions and memories only exist for as long as we keep them alive. If we let go of them, just like exiting a group chat, they disappear. But if we hold onto them, they remain active in our minds, even if no one else remembers them. This is why it's essential to recognize when we're holding onto something unnecessarily. The moment we choose to release that grip, the power they have over us diminishes.

A few years ago, I gave a presentation in class that I felt went horribly wrong. I forgot key points, stumbled through my sentences, and rushed to finish. For days, I replayed it in my head, convinced everyone thought I was incompetent. Weeks later, I brought it up to a classmate. She looked at me blankly and said, "Oh, I don't even remember that day."

That was the moment it clicked. Just like a WhatsApp group where everyone has quietly exited, the moment I mentally leave the embarrassment, it disappears from existence. No one is inside the group anymore. Not even me. So why keep checking it?

But let's also acknowledge an important distinction. This perspective helps us understand that most of the negative emotions we experience and the negative memories we remember, such as embarrassment, regret, and shame, exist only because we choose to keep revisiting them. In reality, if we forget them, they disappear entirely.

How to Handle Negative Emotions

Negative emotions, especially embarrassment and regret, are illusions that we maintain. They don't exist outside of our own thoughts. The WhatsApp group analogy helps us visualize this in a simple way.

However, it's important to recognize that not all negative emotions are this light or fleeting. Some emotional experiences like trauma, loss, or deeply rooted pain require more than just a shift in perspective. They may need time, self-compassion, and support through therapy, journaling, or meaningful conversations. The group exit analogy is not meant to minimize those experiences but to offer a helpful mental tool for the kind of overthinking that keeps small, everyday regrets alive longer than necessary.

In psychology, strategies like cognitive reframing or mindful detachment are often used to manage persistent thoughts. The group chat analogy complements these techniques by offering a simple mental cue. I'm choosing not to engage.

Only you are keeping the memory alive. Imagine making a public mistake. Maybe you spilled coffee on yourself in a meeting. For you, the embarrassment is overwhelming, and you replay the moment over and over. But what about others? They may have noticed for a second, but then they moved on. Within minutes, hours, or at most a day, they've forgotten. The only person keeping the group chat, your embarrassment, active is you. If you exit the memory, it's as if it never happened.

Every time you recall a negative memory, you are re-entering the group. Let's say something embarrassing happened years ago, but you still feel the same shame when you think about it. Why? Because every time you revisit that memory, you re-enter the group chat. The moment you stop opening that chat, stop thinking about that incident, it disappears entirely.

Nobody else cares as much as you think they do. In fact, time naturally helps us forget most awkward moments unless we keep feeding them. The more we revisit a moment, the more we delay that natural fading. So instead of reopening the chat, practice consciously stepping away from it. The less attention you give it, the faster it disappears.

Applying the Group Exit Analogy to Daily Life

Now that we understand the concept, how do we use it to handle emotions better?

Ask yourself: Am I the only one who still cares about this? Chances are, you are. If no one else remembers, why should you?

Decide to exit the group. Consciously tell yourself, this moment is gone. I don't need to keep revisiting it.

When the thought comes back, exit again. If an old memory resurfaces, remind yourself: this only exists because I'm thinking about it. If I stop, it disappears.

Imagine the moment as a chat you can delete. Visualizing it as a WhatsApp group makes it easier to let go. Just as you wouldn't keep scrolling through a useless chat, stop replaying unnecessary memories.

Understanding the group exit analogy is a powerful mental shift. It helps us recognize that negative emotions are not permanent, and they only exist if we keep feeding them. Just as a WhatsApp group vanishes when everyone leaves, an embarrassing or painful memory disappears when we stop holding onto it.

Let's take some short examples to understand it better.

Imagine you once stuttered during a presentation, and it still haunts you. But ask yourself, does anyone else even remember it? The group chat of that moment has been empty for a long time. Exit it.

Here's another example. Let's say you made a typing error in an email and felt embarrassed. For you, it was a big deal. For your colleagues? They probably read it, moved on, and never thought about it again. You're the last person in the group chat. Leave, and it's gone.

Now imagine you waved at someone who wasn't waving at you. You felt awkward for days. But what about the other person? They likely forgot within minutes. Exit the group, and the moment disappears.

After a breakup, it may feel like the world is watching. But in reality, people move on. If you stop replaying the pain, it stops existing. The moment is in the past. The group is empty. Leave it.

Life is full of moments that feel massive but fade quickly in the eyes of others. The more we understand that our negative emotions are often self-sustained, the easier it becomes to move forward. The WhatsApp group analogy doesn't erase the need for emotional growth, but it gives us a helpful mental shortcut. When you're ready, exit the group. Not to deny what happened, but to choose peace over repetition.

Emotional growth doesn't mean pretending something didn't happen. It means reaching a place where it no longer controls your inner world. Some memories may never disappear entirely, but their weight can lighten over time, especially when we're kind to ourselves and, if needed, open to healing support.

* * *

VII

CHAPTER 7: WHAT LEADS TO BETTER RESULTS

This chapter reveals the strategies and approaches that consistently lead to better outcomes. It emphasizes the importance of exposure, trial, and learning from both success and failure to achieve sustainable results.

Perspective 13: The Power of Exposure

In this perspective, we will explore how to improve our results by making strategic shifts in our actions and mindset. Success isn't just about working harder; it's about understanding what truly drives better outcomes. Often, small adjustments in approach, exposure, and timing can create a significant impact on our progress.

Through the next two perspectives, we will uncover key principles that can help you achieve more with less resistance. Whether it's leveraging the power of exposure or mastering the art of the first approach, this chapter will provide insights to enhance your results in both personal and professional life.

Have you ever wondered why the first time you do something feels intimidating, but it becomes easier the second or third time? Whether it's driving, public speaking, or learning a new language, the first attempt always feels the hardest. But with repetition, it slowly becomes second nature. This is the power of consistency and breaking through the initial discomfort. The more you practice, the more familiar and manageable it becomes.

This is not a coincidence, it's the power of exposure at work. Every time you do something, your brain builds neural pathways associated with that action. The first time you attempt a skill, the neural pathway is weak, like a newly paved road with cracks and gaps. But as you repeat the action, the pathway strengthens, becoming like a well-built highway where signals travel faster and more efficiently.

Of course, this analogy simplifies a much more intricate neurological process. In reality, skill development and habit formation involve a web of brain activity. Cognitive processing, emotional associations, feedback loops, and individual learning styles all play a role. But for practical understanding, imagining neural pathways as roads helps us grasp how repeated actions become easier and more automatic over time.

Think about a child learning to walk. At first, every step is unsteady, and falling is inevitable. But with each attempt, their body and brain begin to synchronize, making walking feel natural. This principle applies to every skill in life. The more you expose yourself to a certain task, the better you become at it.

Now, consider something you fear, maybe public speaking, networking, or writing. The primary reason these tasks feel difficult is simply because you haven't been exposed to them enough. The secret to overcoming fear and mastering any skill is controlled, repeated exposure.

This perspective explains why people who practice more tend to outperform those who don't. It also highlights why deliberate exposure to difficult situations is key to growth. Just like practice makes perfect, exposure makes mastery inevitable.

Neural Pathways and Familiarity: The Science Behind Exposure

The brain is like a muscle; it strengthens through use. When you're exposed to something new, your neurons must work harder to process the information. The first time you do something, your brain struggles because it doesn't yet have an efficient neural pathway for that action. But when you repeat the same action, the neural connections become stronger. Your brain learns from past experiences and adjusts, making the action feel smoother and more natural. This is why the second time you do something is always easier than the first.

Consider learning to drive. The first time behind the wheel, you have to consciously think about every movement, pressing the brake, turning the steering wheel, checking the mirrors. But after weeks or months of practice, driving becomes automatic. Why? Because your brain has strengthened the neural pathways associated with driving.

Exposure Creates Confidence and Reduces Fear

One of the biggest reasons people feel uncomfortable in new situations is unfamiliarity. The brain perceives unknown experiences as potential threats, triggering feelings of anxiety or hesitation. But once the same experience is repeated, the brain realizes there's no actual danger, reducing fear and increasing confidence.

For example, imagine someone terrified of public speaking. Their hands shake, their voice trembles, and their mind goes blank. But what happens if they expose themselves to speaking in front of a mirror every day? After a few days, the fear slightly reduces. Then they try speaking in front of a small group. Over time, they gain confidence, and the same act that once felt terrifying becomes manageable.

This is why exposure therapy is commonly used to treat phobias. By gradually exposing people to their fears in controlled environments, the brain rewires itself to stop perceiving those situations as threats. A related and structured approach to this is systematic desensitization therapy, which builds on the principles of exposure while incorporating relaxation techniques to make the process more manageable.

Practical Applications of Exposure

Exposure is the key to overcoming fear and mastering new skills. Take public speaking, for example. If speaking in front of an audience feels intimidating, start by practicing in front of a mirror. Then record yourself to analyze your delivery. Gradually move on to speaking in front of a friend or a small group. With each step, your confidence grows, making public speaking feel natural over time.

The same principle applies to networking and social skills. If socializing makes you anxious, begin with small, low-pressure interactions, greeting a cashier or making small talk with a barista. These small moments of exposure help build comfort, making larger conversations and networking events much easier. Over time, you'll gain more confidence, and these interactions will become second nature. As your comfort level increases, you can gradually challenge yourself with bigger social scenarios.

Writing and creativity also thrive on exposure. Many people struggle with writing simply because they don't do it enough. By making writing a daily habit, whether it's journaling, drafting ideas, or free-writing, the brain becomes more fluent in processing thoughts and expressing them clearly. Over time, what once felt difficult becomes second nature.

Similarly, physical skills like sports, dancing, or playing an instrument can feel awkward at first. The initial attempts may be clumsy, but continued exposure builds muscle memory and coordination. With each practice session, movements become smoother and reflexes sharper, proving that consistent exposure is the foundation of mastery.

Why People Struggle Despite Understanding This Concept

Many people fail to use the power of exposure because they expect immediate results. They try something once or twice, feel uncomfortable, and then assume they're not good at it. But discomfort is a natural part of the learning process.

Another reason people struggle is that they don't expose themselves to challenges regularly. For example, if someone speaks in public once a year, they won't develop confidence. But if they do it once a week, their brain will adjust much faster.

The Dark Side of Exposure

The power of exposure can be a tool for growth and progress, but it can also lead to negative patterns and destructive behaviours. Just as gradual exposure can help people overcome fears and build resilience, it can also make harmful activities feel more normal and acceptable.

Take drug use as an example. The first time someone tries a drug, their brain might initially resist due to fear, uncertainty, or even physical discomfort. But with repeated exposure, the brain starts adapting. The second and third time become easier as the initial hesitation fades and familiarity builds. Confidence grows, and what once seemed dangerous now feels comfortable. This process mirrors how exposure therapy helps rewire the brain—but in this case, it reinforces a harmful habit instead of breaking a fear response.

This is why normal people view drug abusers very differently. Those who are addicted have already gone through gradual exposure over time. The small, seemingly insignificant exposures they experienced earlier in life have accumulated, making their current situation drastically different from that of an average person. For an addict, what they're doing might feel "normal" or even necessary, while to a regular person, the same behaviour appears extreme and self-destructive. The reason for this gap in perception is that an addict's exposure levels have escalated far beyond what a non-user can relate to. This concept is also covered in the last perspective, The Tunnel Analogy, where small, unnoticed steps gradually lead someone deeper into a reality that seems natural to them but is shocking to those outside of it.

Over time, repeated exposure can lead to tolerance, dependence, and eventually addiction, as the brain increasingly craves the substance to achieve the same effect. The same principle applies to other negative behaviours, such as gambling, excessive social media use, or unhealthy relationships. What starts as discomfort or hesitation can, through repeated exposure, turn into a deeply ingrained habit.

Understanding this concept is crucial because it reminds us that exposure itself is not inherently good or bad—it depends on what we're exposing ourselves to. By being mindful of where we direct our repeated experiences, we can use the power of exposure to build positive habits rather than falling into destructive cycles.

Exposure itself is neutral. It's a force that amplifies what we repeatedly experience, whether positive or negative. The power of exposure is undeniable; it shapes our perceptions, builds our confidence, and determines what we see as normal or acceptable. Whether for personal growth or destructive habits, repeated exposure rewires the brain in ways that can be beneficial or harmful.

This is why being intentional about what we expose ourselves to is crucial. While exposure can help us overcome fears, build resilience, and improve our lives, it can just as easily lead us down a dangerous path if directed toward negative influences.

The gradual process that makes learning a new skill easier is the same process that can make addiction or harmful behaviours feel natural over time.

Recognizing this allows us to take control of our exposure, ensuring that we're reinforcing positive habits instead of unconsciously shaping a reality we may later regret. Ultimately, by understanding how exposure influences our mindset and choices, we can harness its power for growth while avoiding the slow, unnoticed descent into destructive patterns.

* * *

Perspective 14: The First Approach Strategy

Welcome to the 14th perspective! This chapter is all about the power of taking the first step. Whether in relationships, opportunities, or personal growth, the way we initiate action often determines the outcome. Here, we'll explore why the First Approach Strategy works, how it influences productivity, and how applying it to different areas of life can lead to significantly better results.

Imagine two students assigned a 100-page research paper. The first student starts slow, writing just a page or two in the first week, thinking they have plenty of time. As the deadline nears, they scramble to finish, facing overwhelming pressure and exhaustion. The second student, however, begins with intensity, completing 20 pages in the first two days. With a solid foundation already in place, they can pace themselves comfortably and submit a well-researched, stress-free paper.

This difference highlights the essence of the First Approach Strategy. The way you begin a task significantly impacts your long-term success. If you start with momentum, focus, and intensity, you set yourself up for consistent progress. But if you start slow, you risk falling into procrastination, delays, and unnecessary stress.

This strategy applies to almost every area of life. Whether it is starting a business, preparing for an exam, or launching a new habit, the initial effort builds momentum and makes the rest of the journey easier and more efficient.

Most people underestimate the power of a strong start. They assume there is plenty of time and adopt a relaxed approach, only to regret it when pressure builds. In contrast, those who begin with full energy and commitment gain an early advantage that carries them forward with less resistance.

The Science Behind a Strong Start

When we begin something new, our brain is especially engaged and receptive. This phenomenon, known as the "fresh start effect," describes how people feel more motivated at the beginning of a new project, job, or habit. If you leverage this energy effectively, you can achieve substantial progress before your motivation fades.

Neuroscience shows that early exposure to a challenge activates the brain's prefrontal cortex, which governs focus and decision-making. A powerful first approach strengthens neural pathways, making it easier to maintain productivity. On the other hand, a slow start signals to the brain that the task is not urgent, often leading to procrastination and sluggish progress.

Avoiding the Trap of Procrastination

Many people struggle with procrastination because they start with a relaxed mindset. When you begin slowly, your brain adjusts to low effort, making it harder to switch into high-performance mode later. The First Approach Strategy eliminates this problem by generating momentum right from the start.

For example, if a student starts studying intensely from day one, their brain adapts to the challenge, making continued focus more natural. But if they delay, they must suddenly force their brain into high gear later on, which often feels overwhelming and exhausting.

The Psychological Advantage of Early Progress

Progress itself is a motivator. When you accomplish a significant portion of a task early, you feel a sense of achievement that drives you to continue. People who achieve early wins are more likely to finish their goals successfully.

For instance, imagine an entrepreneur launching a new business. If they secure their first few clients within the first month, their confidence rises and they are more likely to expand. On the other hand, if they struggle to get started, they may lose motivation and abandon the idea altogether.

The First Approach Strategy helps prevent burnout by ensuring that much of the work is completed while motivation is at its peak. This reduces stress and allows for a more strategic and relaxed pace later on. By tackling key tasks early on, it creates a foundation that can be built upon, ensuring consistent progress without overwhelming pressure.

Applying This Strategy in Different Areas of Life

This strategy can be used in many areas to build momentum and make long-term success easier to achieve.

When writing a book or research paper, instead of pacing yourself slowly over several weeks, it is more effective to start with a burst of energy, writing as much as possible in the early days. This early effort creates momentum that makes the rest of the process smoother.

In business, new entrepreneurs should focus on gaining strong traction in the early months by actively marketing, networking, and refining their offerings. A solid start creates a foundation for sustained growth.

The same principle applies to fitness and health goals. Establishing a consistent and intense routine in the beginning helps build lasting habits. Even if motivation fades later, the routine remains ingrained.

When learning a new skill, such as coding, a new language, or an instrument, an immersive beginning accelerates learning. The brain absorbs new information more effectively when exposed to intense and focused practice early on. This initial phase lays a strong foundation, making it easier to build upon later. The deeper the immersion, the quicker the brain adapts.

Why Most People Struggle With This Strategy

The most common mistake people make is underestimating the difficulty of a task. They believe they can catch up later, but that rarely happens. Without a strong start, tasks tend to pile up, leading to stress and a decline in quality.

Another challenge is lack of planning. Many people begin with enthusiasm but no structure, which causes their motivation to fade. The key is to combine a powerful start with a clear action plan to maintain momentum.

If you want to succeed in anything, whether it is work, academics, health, or business, how you start matters more than you think. A weak start sets off a chain reaction of procrastination and panic. A strong start builds momentum, confidence, and steady progress.

This strategy is evident in countless success stories. A college student who wrote 20 pages of a paper within the first two days had a smooth and confident experience, while another student who procrastinated struggled and submitted a rushed assignment. Elon Musk's companies, including Tesla and SpaceX, made rapid progress from the beginning, allowing them to lead their industries. The early momentum they built was crucial in establishing their dominance. A person committed to daily workouts in their first two weeks found it easier to maintain the routine later. Entrepreneurs who focused on aggressive client acquisition early on gained confidence and resources to scale faster, propelling them to greater success.

The First Approach Strategy is not just about working hard. It is about working smart. A focused and intensive start makes the rest of the journey less stressful and more manageable. It builds a strong foundation that supports long-term success.

If you have a goal or project in front of you, do not hesitate or take a cautious pace at the beginning. Start with full force. Significant early progress boosts your confidence and provides a buffer for challenges ahead. Success is not only about persistence; it is about how you begin. Those who give their maximum effort from the very beginning gain the edge that makes all the difference.

* * *

VIII

CHAPTER 8: THE TRUTH ABOUT INTENTIONS

Intentions shape our actions and results. In this final chapter, we dissect the concept of intention, exploring how our true motives impact our decisions and how we can align them with our values to create authentic and meaningful outcomes.

Perspective 15: The Overestimation of Karma

et's jump into the 15th perspective. The concept of karma has been deeply ingrained in human belief systems for centuries. It is often described as the universal law of cause and effect, what you put into the world comes back to you. If you do good, good will return. If you do bad, consequences will follow. While this idea carries truth, many people overestimate karma's role and misunderstand how it actually works.

This perspective challenges the traditional belief that karma alone determines our outcomes. In its original spiritual and philosophical contexts, especially in Hinduism, Buddhism, and Jainism, karma goes far beyond action and reaction. It includes intention, accumulated impressions, and the soul's journey across lifetimes. This chapter isn't meant to dismiss that depth but to focus on how karma is often misunderstood or oversimplified in modern thinking.

In today's world, karma is sometimes treated like a cosmic reward-punishment system based purely on visible actions. That's the version we're addressing here.

Many people believe karma alone determines the outcome of one's life. They assume every good or bad action results in an immediate and equivalent consequence. However, this perception is simplistic and misleading. In reality, karma is just one part of a much bigger picture, and intention plays a far greater role than most people realize.

Consider this: Two people donate money to charity. One genuinely wants to help, while the other wants to appear generous in public. According to the common understanding of karma, both should receive the same positive result. But should they? If karma were solely based on action, both would earn the same return. Yet, the universe often responds to the energy behind an action, not just the action itself.

Intention influences how we approach situations, make decisions, and interact with the world. While actions are important, they are often just external expressions of deeper internal processes. What you think, believe, and intend can have a greater impact on your life than what you do on the surface.

Let's explore why karma is often overestimated and why intention shapes reality more powerfully than we realize.

Why People Overestimate Karma

People overestimate karma because actions are visible and measurable, while intentions remain hidden. Society judges individuals based on what they do, not why they do it. This creates a bias where karma or outward action appears more important than it actually is, overlooking the deeper motivations that drive those actions. As a result, we often miss the true essence behind people's behavior.

Additionally, many people have an instant gratification mindset. They expect immediate rewards for good behaviour, assuming life should deliver equal returns right away. But life rarely works in such predictable patterns. Karma does influence life's fairness, but it is not the sole force at play. Environment, personal growth, and internal alignment also shape our outcomes.

The Legal System Proves Intention Matters More

One of the clearest examples of intention outweighing action is found in the legal system. If karma alone determined consequences, every crime would receive the same punishment. But law distinguishes between intent and outcome.

A person who premeditates a crime receives a harsher sentence than someone who causes harm unintentionally. The difference between murder and manslaughter lies in intent. Similarly, someone who steals food to feed their family is judged differently from someone who steals out of greed. The legal system recognizes that morality is not defined by action alone but by the intention behind it.

The same applies in life. Our inner world, our thoughts, beliefs, and motives, shapes reality more than our external behaviours.

Why Intention Shapes Reality More Than Karma

Intentions are the root of our thoughts, decisions, and actions. They affect our energy, influence our direction, and determine how we experience the world. Even seemingly good actions, if rooted in selfishness or manipulation, often result in negative outcomes. In contrast, pure intentions tend to attract support and success, even when our actions aren't perfect.

I remember when a junior employee once deleted an important file from our team drive. It was a mistake that set us back a few hours. Some people were furious and wanted him reprimanded. But when I spoke to him, he looked devastated.

"I was trying to organize the folders to make things easier for everyone," he said. "I thought I was helping."

In that moment, I saw the difference between karma and intention. His action had a negative result, but his intention was thoughtful and sincere. If we judged him solely by the result, we'd call it incompetence. But when we looked at the intention, we saw kindness misfired.

That's when I understood something deeper: judging people by outcomes alone often hides the truth that only intention can reveal.

The Iceberg Analogy

Karma is like the tip of an iceberg, the part that is visible. But intention is the massive structure beneath the surface, hidden from immediate view. It is what truly determines the direction of our lives. Actions may appear similar, but it's the invisible force of intention that defines long-term impact, shaping outcomes in ways we often don't see at first.

How to Shift Your Focus from Karma to Intention? Real change begins with inner alignment.Understanding that karma is overestimated doesn't mean ignoring it; it means prioritizing intention. When your thoughts and beliefs align with your goals, the right actions follow naturally.

A simple act, like helping someone across the street, can have two entirely different energies. One person might act out of compassion, another for the sake of capturing a video for social media. The action is identical, but the long-term effects and internal growth are worlds apart.

The same holds true in business. One entrepreneur donates money to a cause they believe in and feels deeply fulfilled. Another donates for tax benefits, seeing it as a transaction. Though the action looks the same, the internal experience and ripple effects on reputation, relationships, and future opportunities are completely different.

This also applies to career success. Imagine two people applying for the same job. One believes in themselves. The other doubts their worth. Even if they perform equally well, the confident one is more likely to succeed. Their energy, clarity, and intention will come through in ways the other can't fake. It shows that success isn't just about effort, it's about alignment.

If karma were the only force determining success, many manipulative and dishonest people would always win. But we know that isn't the case. In the long run, your thoughts, beliefs, and intentions shape your reality. Instead of obsessing over what you do, focus on why you do it. Align your inner world with the outcomes you want, and the rest will follow.

But Intention Alone Is Not Enough

Here's something important to recognize. While intention is powerful, it's not enough if you're unaware of the environment and belief systems that shaped those intentions in the first place.

Often, we act not just from intention, but from deeply embedded perspectives—formed by childhood, society, culture, and past experiences. What you believe to be a "good" intention might still be shaped by fear, bias, or conditioning.

And that brings us to a deeper truth: we don't just act from intention, we act from perspective.

The same action can mean very different things depending on the lens through which it's viewed. To fully understand ourselves and others, we need to go beyond karma. We need to go beyond intention.

* * *

Perspective 16: The Tunnel Analogy

Have you ever wondered why different people see the world so differently? Why some behaviours seem completely normal to one person but strange or even wrong to another? The answer lies in perspective, more specifically, the personal "tunnel" through which each of us views life.

In this final perspective, The Tunnel Analogy, we'll explore how every person's worldview is shaped by their upbringing, culture, experiences, and beliefs. Just as standing inside a tunnel limits what you can see, our personal backgrounds shape how we interpret the world around us. Understanding this concept not only helps us make sense of human behaviour but also reduces unnecessary judgment, conflict, and misunderstanding.

Imagine standing at the entrance of a long tunnel, peering inside. The walls stretch ahead, curving in the distance, restricting your view. The only way to understand what lies within is to step inside. Now, imagine every person you meet standing inside their own mental tunnel shaped by upbringing, experiences, achievements, relationships, culture, and more.

This is the Tunnel Analogy, a way of understanding why people see the world differently. Every person's frame of view is unique. Because of this, they see life in a way that makes sense to them, even if it seems strange to someone outside their experience. What feels right, logical, or even necessary to one person might seem completely irrational to another, not because one is right and the other is wrong, but because they are standing in different frames of reference.

But how are these tunnels formed? A tunnel is not built overnight. It begins in childhood, when beliefs are passed down by parents, teachers, and early role models. As we grow, each life event, whether a major success, painful failure, heartbreak, or moment of triumph, adds layers to that tunnel. Think of these experiences as bricks, each one shaping how wide or narrow the tunnel becomes, how light or dark it feels inside, and how far you can see. Some outlooks are open and expansive, shaped by diverse experiences. Others are tight and limiting, formed by trauma, isolation, or rigid belief systems.

One of the biggest mistakes we make in life is assuming that everyone sees the world the same way we do. This assumption leads to misunderstandings, conflicts, and misjudgments. The Tunnel Analogy helps explain why people have different perspectives and why certain behaviours may seem normal to one person but strange or even wrong to another.

For instance, cultural differences exist because each society operates within its own interpretive lens. What is considered polite in one country may be seen as rude in another. Similarly, people often judge others without realizing that their judgments are based on their own worldview, not an objective truth. Something that seems weird or wrong to one person might be completely normal to another simply because they come from different backgrounds. Even in cases of criminal behaviour, the life framework a person grows up in can shape their sense of right and wrong. Someone raised in poverty or violence might justify actions that others see as unacceptable.

Of course, understanding someone's tunnel does not mean you have to agree with or excuse their behaviour, but it does mean you approach it with insight instead of immediate judgment. The mistake we often make is believing that everyone is standing in the same tunnel as us. We assume our perspective is the default or the correct one. However, true understanding comes from recognizing that every person's inner framework is different.

Every Person Stands in a Different Tunnel

No two people experience life in exactly the same way because each individual's perspective is shaped by a unique combination of factors. Our upbringing plays a major role. Parents, teachers, friends, and society instill values and beliefs from an early age, shaping how we see the world. Cultural background also influences our thinking, as traditions and customs vary widely across different societies. Additionally, life experiences such as failures, successes, trauma, or achievements contribute to the formation of our personal viewpoint. Even two siblings who grow up in the same household can have completely different outlooks because they encounter different challenges, friendships, and influences. In the end, every person's perspective is a complex blend of all these elements, making it uniquely their own.

You can think of tunnels as mental filters. They determine what gets noticed, what gets dismissed, and how events are interpreted. Recognizing this can be a game changer in personal relationships, professional settings, and even global affairs.

For example, a person raised in a highly competitive environment may see success as the only option, believing that life is about winning. Meanwhile, another person raised in a more relaxed, supportive environment may value happiness over achievement, seeing personal fulfillment as more important than external success. Both perspectives make sense within their respective lived realities, but if these two individuals judge each other without understanding their backgrounds, they will likely see the other as wrong.

Why We Misjudge Others

One of the main reasons for misunderstandings in life is that people assume others see the world the same way they do. When someone behaves differently, we often judge them based on our own tunnel rather than considering their perspective.

Take the example of someone wearing flashy, extravagant clothing and acting loudly in public. From one perspective, this person might seem like they are seeking attention. However, in their own reference point, this could be completely normal. Perhaps they grew up in a culture where being expressive was encouraged, or maybe their background made them value standing out rather than blending in. What seems loud to one person might feel authentic to another. Judging them without understanding their life lens would lead to an unfair assumption.

Cultural misunderstandings also illustrate this concept. In some cultures, direct eye contact is considered a sign of confidence and respect. In others, it may be seen as aggressive or disrespectful. If someone from a culture that values eye contact interacts with someone from a culture that avoids it, they might perceive the other as rude or dishonest when, in reality, it is simply a difference in cultural norms.

Even in more serious cases, such as criminal behaviour, the Tunnel Analogy helps explain why people make certain choices. Many individuals who engage in crime do not necessarily see themselves as bad people. Their life environment, shaped by poverty, violence, or survival instincts, may have led them to believe that certain actions are necessary. A person who grows up in an environment where theft is a means of survival will view stealing differently than someone raised in a stable, privileged background.

This does not mean we accept all actions as justifiable, but it does mean we understand that behaviour is often the result of a personal context, not just a decision. This mindset promotes reform, dialogue, and compassion instead of blame.

The Power of Seeing the Whole Tunnel

Most people only see the world from inside their own tunnel, but those who seek understanding look at the entire structure. Instead of judging someone based on a single action or belief, they try to understand the experiences and influences that shaped that person's perspective.

This ability to step outside one's own tunnel is what makes great leaders, psychologists, and empathetic individuals stand out. They recognize that perspectives are shaped by environment, upbringing, and culture, which allows them to connect with a diverse range of people. When you take the time to understand where someone is coming from, you reduce unnecessary conflicts caused by misinterpretations. Instead of reacting emotionally to someone's actions, you begin to see the logic behind their behaviour.

Moreover, by exposing people to new ideas and experiences, we can help expand their inner perspective. A person who has never travelled may have a narrow view of the world, but once they experience different cultures, their worldview expands. The more perspectives we are exposed to, the wider our mental scope becomes, making it easier to navigate the complexities of human interaction.

How to Expand Your Own Tunnel

The more experiences you have, the more flexible and understanding your perspective becomes. A narrow tunnel leads to rigid thinking, while an expanded frame of mind allows for greater empathy and adaptability. As you grow and encounter diverse situations, your ability to see beyond the obvious deepens.

To broaden your tunnel:

- Travel to unfamiliar places and immerse yourself in different cultures.
- Read books and listen to stories from people with backgrounds unlike yours.
- Engage in open conversations with those who challenge your views.
- Reflect on your own mental blueprint. What experiences, beliefs, or biases may be shaping your view without your awareness?

Instead of immediately dismissing views that contradict your own, try to understand what shaped them. Every time you do this, your perception range expands. You create more room for nuance, and that makes you a wiser thinker and a better human being.

The more you step outside your own experiences, the more you realize that life is not about finding one universal truth. It is about understanding that different lenses exist, each making sense in its own way to the people within them.

The Tunnel Analogy offers a powerful way to understand human behaviour and reduce unnecessary judgment. Everyone is shaped by their own experiences, culture, and upbringing, which means that no two people see life in exactly the same way. By recognizing that we all live in different tunnels, we can become more understanding, open-minded, and adaptable.

Expanding your own mental model through travel, reading, and conversations will not only help you see the world differently but also allow you to connect with people on a deeper level. The more you step outside your own tunnel, the more you will realize that life is not about proving your perspective is the only right one. It is about understanding the perspectives of others and learning to navigate the world with greater wisdom and empathy.

The world is not a single road where everyone walks the same path. It is a network of distinct realities, each shaped by unique life experiences. If you want to grow, do not just stay inside your own tunnel. Explore others, understand them, and expand your view of the world. Because at the end of the day, true wisdom is not about proving your tunnel is the best. It is about recognizing that everyone's tunnel has its own story, and every story matters.

* * *

Final Reflection

You've now explored sixteen distinct ways of seeing the world, each one offering a shift, a crack in the usual way of thinking. Some of these ideas may have resonated deeply, while others might challenge you later at unexpected moments. That is the thing about perspective. It doesn't always demand agreement, but it often leaves behind a question that lingers.

You might already be familiar with some of these perspectives. Perhaps you've even lived them in your own way. But there is a difference between knowing something and truly seeing it. Sometimes it takes a new angle, a simple reframing, for an idea to land in a way that sticks. That is the beauty of shifting perspective. It does not demand instant change. It invites curiosity. And when curiosity replaces judgment, real growth begins.

If you are going through something heavy, know that you are not alone. Seeking help is not weakness. It is strength in motion. In fact, seeking help is a powerful shift in itself. It shows awareness, courage, and a willingness to move forward. Please consider speaking to a qualified professional if you are dealing with something that needs support. Your mental and emotional well-being matters, and taking care of it is part of walking this path with clarity.

This is not the end of your journey. It is the beginning of a new way of thinking. So keep questioning. Keep noticing. Keep reflecting. And most of all, keep shifting. Because sometimes the smallest shift in perspective changes everything.

* * *

What's Next?

Thank you for reading *Shift Your Perspective*! This book is just the beginning of your journey toward seeing life differently. If you're interested in diving deeper into mindset shifts and personal growth, here's how you can stay connected:

Join The Perspective Shift Club

Scan the QR code below to be part of a community of like- minded individuals focused on personal growth and shifting perspectives.

Or visit: www.paraspanjwani.com/the-perspective-club

About the Author

Paras Panjwani has always been fascinated by the way people think and the perspectives that shape their lives. Through his interdisciplinary studies in Canada, he explored psychology and human behaviour. Inspired by what he learned in Harvard Health Publishing's Positive Psychology, he began applying perspective-shift strategies in real life and saw powerful changes, focusing on well-being, resilience, and personal growth. He examines how mindset shifts can transform the way we live, think, and grow.

Follow on Instagram:

For regular insights on mindset shifts
and personal growth: @paras.panjwani

Visit Website:

Learn more and stay connected: www.paraspanjwani.com